Privacy: A Very Short Introduction

VERY SHORT INTRODUCTIONS are for anyone wanting a stimulating and accessible way into a new subject. They are written by experts, and have been translated into more than 40 different languages.

The series began in 1995, and now covers a wide variety of topics in every discipline. The VSI library now contains over 350 volumes—a Very Short Introduction to everything from Psychology and Philosophy of Science to American History and Relativity—and continues to grow in every subject area.

Very Short Introductions available now:

For more information visit our website

www.oup.com/vsi/

Raymond Wacks

PRIVACY

A Very Short Introduction
SECOND EDITION

OXFORD
UNIVERSITY PRESS

OXFORD
UNIVERSITY PRESS

Great Clarendon Street, Oxford, OX2 6DP,
United Kingdom

Oxford University Press is a department of the University of Oxford.
It furthers the University's objective of excellence in research, scholarship,
and education by publishing worldwide. Oxford is a registered trade mark of
Oxford University Press in the UK and in certain other countries

© Raymond Wacks 2010, 2015

The moral rights of the author have been asserted

First edition published 2010
This edition published 2015

Published in the United States of America by Oxford University Press
198 Madison Avenue, New York, NY 10016, United States of America

British Library Cataloguing in Publication Data
Data available

Library of Congress Control Number: 2014951367

ISBN 978-0-19-872594-7

Printed and bound by
CPI Group (UK) Ltd, Croydon, CR0 4YY

Links to third party websites are provided by Oxford in good faith and
for information only. Oxford disclaims any responsibility for the materials
contained in any third party website referenced in this work.

Contents

Preface

Once upon a time, we boarded an aircraft without a search. Hacking described a cough—probably caused by a virus; and cookies were to be eaten rather than feared. Our world has changed almost beyond recognition. In the four years since the first edition of this book appeared, ample proof has emerged of the mounting fragility of privacy. Surveillance by the state has become almost commonplace. The collection of personal information by private companies occurs on an industrial scale. The advent of Big Data, the Cloud, and other technological advances, some still inchoate, pose grave—some would say lethal—dangers to the survival of privacy.

These disquieting perils seem to intensify daily. Not only are our online activities increasingly vulnerable, novel challenges are presented by closed circuit TV (CCTV) surveillance, innovations in biometrics, radio frequency identification (RFID) systems, smart identity cards, and manifold anti-terrorist measures. The disconcerting explosion of private data through the growth of blogs, social networking sites, such as Facebook, YouTube, MySpace, Twitter, and other contrivances of our digital age render simple generalizations about the significance of privacy problematic. The Web has transformed the Internet from an information provider to a community creator. The manner in which data are collected, stored, exchanged, and used has changed forever—and, with it, the character of the threats to individual privacy. But while the electronic revolution touches almost every part of our lives, it is not, of course, the new technology that is the villain, rather the uses to which it is put.

Private lives may also be destroyed in the hot pursuit of scandal or gossip which is seldom justified by a genuine public interest in its publication.

These matters are at the heart of our concerns about the decay of privacy. But the concept of privacy intrudes into several other important aspects of contemporary life. Perhaps understandably, it is deployed to defend freedom of choice in what are—rightly—regarded as 'private' decisions, especially in free societies: contraception, abortion, and sexuality. Yet, in my writings over the last forty years, I have resisted this promiscuous extension of privacy to these so-called 'decisional' issues, and its conflation with freedom and autonomy. Indeed, in the ever-increasing dystopian prognoses of privacy's decline, rarely is mention made of these concerns. Privacy advocates seldom agonize about these questions, vital though they are, when they warn of the countless dangers posed by our information society. Does this constitute a tacit acknowledgment that the true meaning of privacy corresponds with our intuitive understanding and use of the concept? Is privacy, as I have contended, not primarily an interest in protecting personal information? When we lament its demise, do we not mourn the loss of control over intimate facts about ourselves? And is not the essence of that control the explicit exercise of autonomy in respect of our most intimate particulars, whether they be pried upon or gratuitously published?

My approach may, of course, be mistaken. Why should disparate privacy rights be unable to co-exist as different, but related, dimensions of the same fundamental idea? Why not allow 'informational privacy' to live in peace with 'decisional privacy'? Ironically, I think that the lop-sided neglect of the former and constitutional acceleration of the latter by the United States Supreme Court may now have come full circle, and that there are small signs of a belated recognition of the urgent need legally to protect personal information along European lines, as described in the pages that follow. Unfortunately, however, the concept of 'private life' as formulated by Article 8 of the European Convention on Human Rights, is no less nebulous than Warren and Brandeis's 'right to be let alone'. And the European Court of Human Rights is content that it should be so. Hence, to take only one instance, it has acknowledged that Article 8 protects the right to sleep: confirmation of the immense scope of this provision. To inflate rights in this manner is, I believe, to diminish them.

It is important to clarify that my resistance to equating privacy and autonomy springs neither from a denial of the importance of these freedoms nor from any hostility to the protection of rights, or even their formulation in broad terms to facilitate their legal recognition. It rests instead on the belief that by addressing the problem as the protection of personal information, the pervasive difficulties that are generally forced into the straitjacket of privacy might more readily be resolved. The concept of privacy has become too imprecise and unwieldy an idea to perform useful analytical work. This ambiguity has actually undermined the importance of this value and encumbered its effective protection.

My association with privacy and data protection has largely been from a legal perspective. But, although the law is an indispensable instrument in the protection of privacy, the subject obviously teems with a number of other dimensions, social, cultural, political, psychological, and philosophical, and I attempt in this little book to consider these, along with several other forces that shape our understanding of this perplexing concept.

When I first embarked on this voyage many moons ago, both the literature (predominantly American) and the legislation (principally Scandinavian) were thin on the ground. The first generation of data-protection laws was still embryonic. Since those innocent days the position has, of course, undergone a tectonic shift. My foray into the field originated as an academic exercise to elucidate the complex notion of privacy. But the practical dimensions of this increasingly vulnerable right were never far away. Nor could they be; the Information Age was looming. The binary universe and its manifold digital incarnations along with new, sophisticated electronic surveillance devices and an audaciously invasive media rendered any complacency about the security of personal information rashly ingenuous. In any event, any excessively theoretical delusions were soon extinguished by the law reform bodies and other committees on which I have been fortunate to serve. The experience that I have gained from these opportunities has exerted a powerful influence on my understanding of, and judgment about, the protection of privacy and personal data.

I am grateful, once again, to all at Oxford University Press who have aided and abetted this project. Especial thanks are due to Emma Ma, Deborah Protheroe, Joy Mellor, and Gillian Northcott Liles. After putting the finishing touches to the manuscript—and even while reading the proofs—accounts of invasions have proliferated incessantly. In fact, as I type these words a new privacy controversy has just exploded. Reader, be warned: the subject of this book is highly volatile. Countless fresh challenges to personal privacy lie in wait. Protecting and preserving this fundamental democratic ideal demands relentless vigilance and determination.

Raymond Wacks

List of illustrations

Chapter 1
Privacy in peril

Scarcely a day passes without reports of yet another onslaught on our privacy. Our brave new digital world has all but annihilated a right we once took for granted. The ubiquity of Big Brother no longer shocks. 'Low-tech' collection of transactional data in both the public and private sector has become commonplace. In addition to the routine surveillance by closed circuit TV (CCTV) in public places, the monitoring of mobile telephones, the workplace, vehicles, electronic communications, and online activity has swiftly become widespread in most advanced societies.

In the late 18th century, the Utilitarian philosopher and law reformer, Jeremy Bentham, developed the idea of the 'Panopticon'—a building that enabled a single guard to observe the inmates of an institution unawares: the mere fact that they know they may be under surveillance results in their acting is if they were. This would ensure, he argued, that they conducted themselves appropriately. The concept is invoked figuratively by the French social theorist, Michel Foucault, in his celebrated book, *Discipline and Punish*, to describe contemporary 'disciplinary' society's proclivity to observe and 'normalize'. The Panopticon, in his view, generates an awareness of perpetual visibility as a form of power and domination—without the need for locks and chains. It extends beyond prisons to all hierarchical institutions such as schools, hospital, the army, and so on.

Our privacy is increasingly under siege, though the concept of 'privacy' extends beyond these sorts of intrusions whose principal pursuit is personal information. It is invoked to include a multiplicity of incursions into the private domain—especially by the government—captured in the celebrated slogan, 'the right to be let alone'. This phrase (employed by Warren and Brandeis in their seminal 1890 *Harvard Law Review* article) is redolent of the no less famous 17th century declaration by Sir Edward Coke that 'a man's house is his castle', and has come to embrace an extensive assortment of invasions that encroach not only upon 'spatial' and 'locational' privacy, but also interfere with 'decisional' matters often of a moral character such as abortion, contraception, and sexual preference.

However, these questions, central though they are to freedom of choice and individual autonomy, are not fundamental to the idea of privacy. In *Nineteen Eighty Four*, on the other hand, George Orwell's portrayal of a terrifying surveillance state is vividly realized in his description of a simple room which Winston (mistakenly) believes is free from the eyes of Big Brother:

> It seemed to him that he knew exactly what it felt like to sit in a room like this, in an armchair beside an open fire with your feet in the fender and a kettle on the hob: utterly alone, utterly secure, with nobody watching you, no voice pursuing you, no sound except the singing of the kettle and the friendly ticking of the clock.

It is this shelter from observation that, I suggest, lies at the heart of the most cogent and the most compelling conception of privacy. The true meaning of privacy corresponds with our intuitive understanding and use of this fundamental democratic value. Privacy is, above all, a concern to protect sensitive information. When we lament its demise, we mourn the loss of control over intimate facts about ourselves. And the essence of that control is the explicit exercise of control over of our most intimate facts about us, whether they be pried upon or gratuitously published or disclosed.

This core feature of individual privacy is captured in other similar dystopian depictions of totalitarian societies such as Aldous Huxley's *Brave New World*; Philip K. Dick's *A Scanner Darkly, Eye in the Sky*, and *Ubik*; Paul J. McAuley's *Whole Wide World*; David Brin's *Earth*; Charles Stross's *Glasshouse*; and, most recently, *The Circle* by Dave Eggers. There are also countless films with similar themes of surveillance and totalitarianism such as *Brazil, Conversations, Minority Report, The Truman Show, Enemy of the State, Code 46*, and *Gattaca*.

In the case of surveillance, a moment's reflection will reveal some of its many ironies—and difficulties. Its nature—and our reaction to it—is neither straightforward nor obvious. Is 'Big Brother is Watching You' a threat, a statement of fact, or merely mendacious intimidation? Does it make any difference? Is it the knowledge that I am being observed by, say, a CCTV camera, that violates my privacy? What if the camera is a (now widely available) imitation that credibly simulates the action of the genuine article: flashing light, probing lens, menacing swing? Nothing is recorded, but I am unaware of its innocence. What is my objection? Or suppose the camera is real, but faulty—and no images are made, stored, or used? My actions have not been monitored, yet subjectively my equanimity has been disturbed. The mere presence of a device that appears to be observing and recording my behaviour is surely tantamount to its being there in reality.

In other words, it is the *belief* that I am being watched that is my grievance. It is immaterial whether I am in fact the subject of surveillance. My objection is therefore not that I am being observed—for I am not—but the possibility that I may be (see Figure 1).

In this respect, being watched by a visible CCTV camera differs from that other indispensable instrument of the spy: the electronic listening device. When my room or office is bugged, or my telephone is tapped, I am—by definition—usually oblivious to this

3

1. A common misconception about the right to privacy.

infringement of my privacy. Yet my ignorance does not, of course, render the practice inoffensive. Unlike the case of the fake or non-functioning camera, however, I *have* been subjected to surveillance: my private conversations have been recorded or intercepted, albeit unconsciously. The same would be true of the surreptitious interception of my correspondence: email or snail mail.

In the former case, no personal information has been obtained; in the latter, it has, but I may never know. Both practices are subsumed in the category of 'intrusion', yet each exhibits a distinctive apprehension. Indeed, the more one examines this (neglected) problem, the less cohesive the subject of 'intrusion' becomes. Each activity requires a separate analysis; each entails a discrete set of concerns, though they are united in a general anxiety that one's society may be approaching, or already displays features of, the Orwellian horror of relentless scrutiny.

As with Bentham's Panopticon, the question is fundamentally one of perception and its consequences. Although my conviction that I am being monitored by CCTV is based on palpable evidence, and my ignorance of the interception of my correspondence or conversations is plainly not, the discomfort is similar. In both cases, it is the distasteful recognition that one needs to adjust one's behaviour—on the assumption that one's words or deeds are being monitored. During the darkest years of repression in apartheid

South Africa, for example, the telephones of anti-government activists were routinely tapped by the security services. One's conversations were therefore conducted with circumspection and trepidation. This inevitably rendered dialogue stilted and unnatural. It is this requirement to adapt or adjust one's behaviour in public (in the case of CCTV) or in private (on the telephone, in one's home, or online) that is the disquieting result of a state that fails properly to regulate the exercise of surveillance.

Privacy and state surveillance

In 2010, when the first edition of this book was in press, the now famous (or infamous) international, online, journalistic NGO (non-governmental organization), Wikileaks, led by Julian Assange, began releasing a huge number of documents relating, in the main, to the wars in Afghanistan and Iraq. They included a video of an airstrike in Baghdad which had resulted in the death of several Iraqi journalists almost 80,000 previously classified documents about that war; and 779 secret files concerning prisoners detained at the Guantanamo prison camp. Towards the end of that year it released almost 400,000 secret United States (US) military logs detailing its operations in Iraq, and it collaborated with several media organizations to disclose US State Department diplomatic cables. In 2013, Bradley (now Chelsea) Manning, a 25-year-old soldier, was convicted of twenty charges in connection with the leaks, including espionage, and sentenced to thirty-five years' imprisonment.

But its activities, though continuing, have been eclipsed by the massive revelations in June 2013 by a former US government contractor, Edward Snowden (see Figure 2). In a dramatic sequence of whistle-blowing, he revealed the enormous extent of the surveillance conducted by the National Security Agency (NSA). The first act in the drama was the disclosure by the British newspaper, *The Guardian*, that the NSA was collecting the telephone records of tens of millions of Americans. This was soon followed by the publication of PowerPoint slides by *The Guardian* and the

2. NSA whistle-blower, Edward Snowden.

Washington Post that purported to show that the NSA had direct access—via the PRISM programme—to the servers of several major tech companies, including Apple, Google, and Microsoft. *The Guardian* subsequently exposed the fact that these companies had worked closely with the NSA to assist them in evading encryption and other privacy controls. It disclosed, for instance, that in February 2013 alone the NSA collected almost three billion pieces of intelligence on Americans. Over the ensuing months a string of leaks emanating from Snowden were released by both newspapers divulging the massive scope of surveillance undertaken, not only by the NSA, but by security services in numerous countries. They included disclosures of spying by both the US and Britain on foreign leaders, and the storage by the NSA of domestic communications that contain foreign intelligence information; the suggestion of a crime; threats of serious harm to life or property; or any other evidence that could advance its electronic surveillance—including encrypted communications. Moreover, it emerged that, since December 2012, the NSA has the capacity to collect a trillion metadata records. Other leaks suggested that the US had spied on the European Union (EU) offices in New York, Washington, DC, and Brussels, as well as the embassies of France, Greece, India, Italy, Japan, Mexico, South Korea, and Turkey.

There was more. Evidence in the form of the PowerPoint slides appeared to show the existence of an NSA programme called 'Upstream' that collects information from the fibre optic cables that carry most Internet and phone traffic. Other slides revealed a programme comprising a network of 500 servers scattered across the world that amass almost all online activities conducted by a user, storing the information in databases searchable by name, email, IP address, region, and language. And it divulged that the private sector, including several telecom companies, provide the British security agency, GCHQ, with unrestricted access to their fibre optic cable networks, carrying a vast quantity of Internet and telephone traffic.

In addition, according to these leaks, the NSA has succeeded in cracking the encryption methods widely used by millions of individuals and organizations to protect their email, e-commerce, and financial transactions. It is also alleged that the NSA employs its colossal databases to store metadata, such as email correspondence, online searches, and the browsing history of millions of Internet users for up to a year, regardless of whether they are targets of the agency.

The *Washington Post* claimed that the NSA had collected bulk mobile phone location data on ordinary individuals across the globe. It apparently channels five billion mobile phone location records per day into its immense database. Complex algorithms can use these data to determine, for example, whether two people are together in a crowded city. The newspaper also exposed the fact that the agency obtains access to computer systems by embedding them with malware that facilitates remote access computers—even when they are unconnected to an outside network. It claimed that the US has two data centres in China specifically to insert malware on targeted Chinese computer systems.

The leaks even suggested that data are collected from smartphone apps, and that the NSA has the capacity to implant malware in millions of computers around the world, enabling it to obtain access to users' sensitive data. The automated system employs phishing emails and false versions of popular webpages such as Facebook to infect computers (see under Malware below). Another leak alleged that the NSA collects the contents and metadata from every telephone call made in specific target countries and stores them for 30 days, including calls from US citizens who live, visit, or telephone others abroad.

The international shockwaves generated by Snowden's exposures continue to raise searching questions about the acceptable limits of state surveillance in a democratic society. Recently, Vodafone, one of the world's largest mobile phone groups, disturbingly revealed the existence of secret wires that enable government agencies to monitor all conversations on its networks. It claimed that they are widely used in some of the twenty-nine countries in which it operates in Europe and beyond.

The threat of terrorism cannot be taken lightly, but unless individual privacy is to be wholly extinguished, the effective oversight of security services is indispensable. In March 2014, President Obama announced that the NSA's bulk collection of Americans' telephone records would be terminated. He acknowledged that trust in the intelligence services had been shaken, and pledged to address the concerns of privacy advocates. Leaders of the White House intelligence committee stated that a deal would be struck with the White House to overhaul the surveillance programme.

The constitutionality of the NSA's mass collection of telephone phone records has now been challenged by the American Civil Liberties Union (ACLU). The complaint contends that the dragnet under Section 215 of the Patriot Act infringes the right of privacy protected by the Fourth Amendment, as well as the First Amendment rights of free speech and association. The lawsuit seeks to terminate the agency's mass domestic surveillance, and to require the deletion of all data collected. A federal judge denied the ACLU's motion for a preliminary injunction, and granted the government's motion to dismiss. The ACLU appealed this decision before the US Court of Appeals for the Second Circuit in New York.

In May 2014 the White House published a report recommending that private companies be obliged to disclose the kind of information they gather from their customers online. The report, a response to the Snowden revelations, specifically refers to the terms of service that consumers click on, invariably without reading them, when they sign up for free email accounts or download apps. The report emphasizes mosaic techniques that permit companies who ostensibly collect anonymous data from large groups of users, to identify users' online activities. It proposes the adoption of a number of approaches including a mandatory system that would compel firms to report data breaches.

Big data

A recent development in the field of data collection and storage is the advent of so-called big data, used to describe the exponential increase and availability of data. It is characterized by what has been called the 'three Vs': volume, velocity, and variety. In respect of the first, the volume is a consequence of the ease of storage of transaction-based data, unstructured data streaming in from social media, and the accumulation of sensor and machine-to-machine data. Second, data are streamed at high velocity from radio frequency identification (RFID) tags, sensors, and smart metering. And, third, data assume a multiplicity of forms including structured, numeric data in traditional databases, from line-of-business applications, unstructured text documents, video, audio, email, and financial transactions.

Its advocates claim that it affords opportunities to correlate data in order to combat crime, prevent disease, forecast weather patterns, identify business trends, and so on. Its detractors question the reliability of its correlations, and the interpretation of the results. According to Patrick Tucker, however, 'we have left the big data era and have entered the *telemetric* age...the collection and transfer of data in *real time*, as though sensed.'

Privacy at work

The increasing use of surveillance in the workplace is changing not only the character of that environment, but also the very nature of what we do and how we do it. The knowledge that our activities are, or even may be, monitored undermines our psychological and emotional autonomy:

> Free conversation is often characterized by exaggeration, obscenity, agreeable falsehoods, and the expression of antisocial desires or views not intended to be taken seriously. The unedited quality of conversation is essential if it is to preserve its intimate, personal and informal character.

Indeed, the slide towards electronic supervision may fundamentally alter our relationships and our identity. In such a world, employees are arguably less likely to execute their duties effectively. If that occurs, the snooping employer will, in the end, secure the precise opposite of what he or she hopes to achieve.

Wiretapping

Both landlines and mobile phones are easy prey to the eavesdropper. In the case of the former, the connection is simply a long circuit comprising a pair of copper wires that form a loop. The circuit carrying your conversation flows out of your home through numerous switching stations between you and the instrument on the other end. At any point a snoop can attach a new load to the circuit board, much in the way one plugs in an additional appliance into an extension cord. In the case of wiretapping, that load is a mechanism that converts the electrical circuit back into the sound of your conversation. The chief shortcoming of this primitive form of interception is that the spy needs to know when the subject is going to use the phone. He needs to be at his post to listen in.

A less inconvenient and more sophisticated method is to install a recording device on the line. Like an answering machine, it picks ups the electrical signal from the telephone line and encodes it as magnetic pulses on audiotape. The disadvantage of this method is that the intruder needs to keep the recorder running continuously in order to monitor any conversations. Few cassettes are large enough. Hence a voice-activated recorder provides a more practical alternative. But here too the tape is unlikely to endure long enough to capture the subject's conversations.

The obvious answer is a bug that receives audio information and broadcasts it using radio waves. Bugs normally have diminutive microphones that pick up sound waves directly. The current is sent to a radio transmitter that conveys a signal that varies with the current. The spy sets up a radio receiver in the vicinity that picks up this signal and transmits it to a speaker or encodes it on a tape. A bug with a microphone is especially valuable since it will hear any conversation in the room, regardless of whether the subject is on the phone. A conventional wiretapping bug, however, can operate without its own microphone, since the telephone has one. All the wiretapper needs to do is to connect the bug anywhere along the phone line, since it receives the electrical current directly. Normally, the spy will connect the bug to the wires inside the telephone.

This is the classic approach. It obviates the need for the spy to revisit the site; the recording equipment may be concealed in a van that typically is parked outside the victim's home or office.

Tapping mobile phones requires the interception of radio signals carried from and to the handsets, and converting them back into sound. The analogue mobile phones of the 1990s were susceptible to easy interception, but their contemporary digital counterparts are much less vulnerable. To read the signals, the digital computer bits need to be converted into sound—a fairly complex and expensive operation. But mobile phone calls may be intercepted at the mobile operator's servers, or on a fixed-line section that carries encrypted voice data for wireless communication.

When you call someone on your mobile phone, your voice is digitized and sent to the nearest base station. It transmits it to another base station adjacent to the recipient's via the mobile carrier's switch operators. Between the base stations, transmission of voice data is effected on landlines, as occurs in the case of fixed-line phone calls. It seems that if an eavesdropper listens to such calls over the landline connection segment, mobile phones are not dissimilar to conventional phones—and are just as vulnerable.

Prior to 2011 numerous politicians and celebrities claimed that the voicemail left on their mobile telephones had been hacked into by the British newspaper, the *News of the World*. The newspaper's royal editor and a private investigator were convicted of hacking messages and sentenced to imprisonment. But the practice assumed seismic proportions when, in July 2011, *The Guardian* reported police suspicion that the mobile telephone of murdered teenager, Milly Dowler, had been hacked by the *News of the World*, and that messages had been deleted to liberate space for new voicemail.

The allegations ignited widespread outrage, and, following denunciation from politicians, the newspaper was closed down by its proprietor, Rupert Murdoch, who paid Milly Dowler's parents and various charities more than $4 million in compensation. The outcry generated by the scandal led to the British government establishing a judge-led enquiry into 'the culture, practices, and ethics of the press.'

The terms of reference of the enquiry extended well beyond the specific matter of intercepted voicemail; they required its chairman, Lord Justice Leveson, to investigate a range of associated questions such as the relationship between politicians, the media, and the police, and the extent to which press self-regulation stood in need of reform (see Chapter 4).

The privacy prognosis

The future of surveillance seems daunting. It promises more sophisticated and alarming intrusions into our private lives, including the greater use of biometrics, and sense-enhanced searches such as satellite monitoring, through-the-wall surveillance (TWS) that can penetrate 30 centimetres of concrete and 15 metres beyond that into a room, laser-based molecular scanners that from a distance of 50 metres can penetrate one's body, clothes, or luggage, and 'smart dust' devices—minuscule wireless micro-electromechanical sensors (MEMS) that can detect everything from light to vibrations. These so-called 'motes'—as tiny as a grain of sand—would collect data that could be sent via two-way band radio between motes up to 300 metres away.

As cyberspace becomes an increasingly perilous domain, we learn daily of new, disquieting assaults on its citizens. This slide towards pervasive surveillance coincides with the mounting fears, expressed well before 11 September 2001, about the disconcerting capacity of the new technology to undermine our liberty. Reports of the fragility of privacy have been sounded for at least a century. But in the last decade they have assumed a more urgent form. And here lies a paradox. On the one hand, recent advances in the power of computers have been decried as the nemesis of whatever vestiges of our privacy that still survive. On the other, the Internet is acclaimed as a Utopia. When clichés contend, it is imprudent to expect sensible resolutions of the problems they embody, but between these two exaggerated claims, something resembling the truth probably resides. In respect of the future of privacy at least, there can be little doubt that the questions are changing before our eyes. And if, in the flat-footed domain of atoms, we have achieved only limited success in protecting individuals against the depredations of surveillance, how much better the prospects in our brave new binary world?

To take a recent example, Google has introduced 'Google Glass', a wearable computer that resembles ordinary spectacles. It has a miniature projector, a camera, a microphone, and a touchpad on one side of the device. Users exercise control by voice commands as well as swipes and tabs on the touchpad. With the device linked to the Internet and using Google as well as third-party applications, wearers can see information superimposed on physical scenes. This development has potentially far-reaching consequences for the security of personal information. It could be used for surveillance or to record and broadcast private conversations. If facial recognition is incorporated, anyone within sight of the Glass-wearer could be identified, with details of all online searchable personal data.

When our security is under siege, so—inevitably—is our liberty. However, a world in which our every movement is observed erodes the very freedom this snooping is often calculated to protect. We need to ensure that the social costs of the means employed to enhance security do not outweigh the benefits. Thus, one unsurprising consequence of the installation of CCTV in car parks, shopping centres, airports, and other public places is the displacement of crime: offenders simply go somewhere else. And, apart from the doors this intrusion opens to totalitarianism, a surveillance society can easily generate a climate of mistrust and suspicion; a reduction in the respect for law and those who enforce it; and an intensification of prosecution of offences that are susceptible to easy detection and proof.

Other developments have comprehensively altered basic features of the legal landscape. The law has been profoundly affected and challenged by countless other advances in technology. Computer fraud, identity (ID) theft, and other 'cyber crimes' are touched on later in this chapter.

Developments in biotechnology such as cloning, stem cell research, and genetic engineering provoke thorny ethical questions and confront traditional legal concepts. Proposals to introduce identity cards and biometrics have attracted strong objections in several jurisdictions. The nature of criminal trials has been transformed by the use of both DNA and CCTV evidence.

Orwellian supervision already appears to be alive and well in several countries. Britain, for example, boasts more than four million CCTV cameras in public places: roughly one for every fourteen inhabitants. It also possesses the world's largest DNA database, comprising some 5.3 million DNA samples. The temptation to install CCTV cameras by both the public and private sector is not easy to resist. Data-protection law (discussed in Chapter 5) ostensibly controls its use, but such regulation has not proved especially effective. A radical solution, adopted in Denmark, is to prohibit their use, subject to certain exceptions such as in petrol stations. The law in Sweden, France, and the Netherlands is more stringent than in the United Kingdom (UK). These countries adopt a licensing system, and the law requires that warning signs be placed on the periphery of the zone monitored. German law has a similar requirement.

But we cannot ignore the impact of the private sector in its pursuit of our personal information. The divide between the state and business is disintegrating. Information is routinely shared between the two. For example, Google may provide user data when subject to a court order. Or even without it. It is claimed that in the US profitable arrangements exist by which the state outsources data gathering to ten major telecommunications companies, including AT&T, Verizon, and T-Mobile who reap considerable sums of money supplying law enforcement authorities with personal telecom information.

More disturbing, however, is the scale of the systematic collection of personal data by major websites such as Google, Facebook, and Amazon. And they frequently comply with government requests for consumers' personal information:

> These companies track one's every keystroke, every order and bill payment one makes, every word and/or phrase in one's emails, even one's every mobile movement through GPS tracking. Data capture involves everything from your personal Social Security number, phone calls, arrest record, credit card transactions and online viewing preferences as well as your medical and insurance records and even personal prescriptions.

Smartphones and other wireless devices are two-way technologies. They contain uploaded personal data that is susceptible to misuses, and they are besieged by downloaded spam. Downloading 'free' apps, including games, often admits a Trojan horse (see under Malware below).

Companies such as PayPal and Visa track online transactions. Google and other agencies obtain private information by cookies and 'click-throughs'. And so-called private data aggregators (e.g. Intelius, Lexis Nexis, and ChoicePoint) collect personal data which they sell.

Biometrics

We are all unique. Your fingerprint is a 'biometric': the measurement of biological information. Fingerprints have long been used as a means of linking an individual to a crime, but they also provide a practical method of privacy protection: instead of logging into your computer with a (not always safe) password, increasing use is being made of fingerprint readers as a considerably more secure entry point. We are likely to see greater use of fingerprint readers at supermarket checkouts and ATMs.

There is no perfect biometric, but the ideal is to find a unique personal attribute that is immutable or, at least, unlikely to change over time. A measurement of this characteristic is then employed as a means of identifying the individual in question. Typically, several samples of the biometric are provided by the subject; they are digitized and stored on a database. The biometric may then be used either to identify the subject by matching his or her data against that of a number of other individuals' biometrics, or to validate the identity of a single subject.

In order to counter the threat of terrorism, we shall unquestionably witness an increased use of biometrics. This includes a number of measures of human physiography as well as DNA. Among the following examples of characteristics on which biometric technologies can be based are one's appearance (supported by still images), e.g. descriptions used in passports, such as height, weight, colour of skin, hair, and eyes, visible physical markings, gender, race, facial hair, the wearing of glasses; natural physiography, e.g. skull measurements, teeth and skeletal injuries, thumbprint, fingerprint sets, handprints, iris and retinal scans, earlobe capillary patterns, heart-beat, hand geometry; biodynamics, e.g. the manner in which one's signature is written, statistically analysed voice characteristics, keystroke dynamics, particularly login-ID and password; social behaviour (supported by video-film), e.g. habituated body signals, general voice characteristics, style of speech, gait, visible handicaps; imposed physical characteristics, e.g. dog-tags, collars, bracelets and anklets, barcodes, embedded microchips, and transponders.

Anxieties have been expressed about a facial recognition database being developed by the Federal Bureau of Investigation (FBI) that could contain 52 million images. The Electronic Frontier Foundation (EFF) has expressed concern that images of non-criminals would be stored alongside those of criminals. The database is part of the bureau's 'Next Generation Identification' (NGI) programme, a large biometric database which will replace the current Integrated Automated Fingerprint Identification System (IAFIS). It is being developed to include the capture and storage of fingerprints, iris scans, and palm prints. There is a fear that biometrics may be used in a way that undermines individual privacy. Biometrics providers will thrive by selling their technology to repressive governments, and establish a foothold in relatively free countries by seeking soft targets; they may start with animals or with captive populations such as the frail, the poor, the old, prisoners, employees, and so on. A less gloomy scenario is that societies will recognize the gravity of the threat and enforce constraints on technologies and their use. This would require public support and the courage of elected representatives who will need to resist pressure from both large corporations and national security and law enforcement authorities, who invoke the bogeymen of terrorism, illegal immigration, and domestic 'law and order' to justify the implementation of this technology.

The Internet

Our life online is increasingly vulnerable—not only to hackers and malicious software, but also to surveillance, tracking, monitoring, and profiling by both the state and businesses. The state's primary interest is in security, while the principal objective of business is obviously the procurement of money. Each requires personal data, normally on a large scale, in order to achieve their respective ends. The result is a diminution of the user's privacy—sometimes with devastating consequences. Surfing the web, anonymously if necessary, using a search engine, entering into online transactions, sending and receiving email—all these quotidian activities—are seriously impaired if we are subjected to monitoring, whether it is a website that tracks our purchases or the security service that intercepts our messages.

Malware

The artillery of malicious software (or 'malware') includes viruses, worms, Trojan horses, spyware, 'phishing', 'bots', 'zombies', and bugs. A virus is a block of code that introduces copies of itself into other programs. It normally carries a payload, which may have only nuisance value, though in many cases the consequences are serious. In order to evade early detection, viruses may delay the performance of functions other than replication. A worm generates copies of itself over networks without infecting other programs. A Trojan horse is a program that appears to carry out a positive task (and sometimes does so), but is often nasty, for instance, keystroke recorders embedded in utilities.

For example, a pernicious bug, dubbed 'Heartbleed'—which had been undetected for years—recently exposed a major flaw in the widely used OpenSSL cryptographic (whose code was thought to be particularly secure) providing access to the memory of the systems protected by the vulnerable versions of the OpenSSL software. It compromises the secret keys used to identify the Internet service providers (ISPs), and to encrypt the traffic, the names and passwords of the users, and the actual content. The bug enables attackers to snoop on communications, steal data directly from the servers and users, and to impersonate them. It has even been alleged that the US National Security Agency (NSA) was aware of the Heartbleed bug as long ago as 2012, and may have exploited the weakness to gather intelligence.

Communications service providers (CSPs) are required, under an EU regulation of 2013, to report all data breaches to regulators within twenty-four hours, and to notify data subjects 'without undue delay' when the breach is 'likely to adversely affect the personal data or privacy' of that individual.

The EU's Article 29 Working Party has since issued guidance on when data controllers should alert data subjects to a personal data breach that is likely to affect their privacy. This obligation extends beyond the advent of bugs such as Heartbleed to include loss of laptops containing medical data and financial data; web vulnerabilities exposing life assurance and medical data; unauthorized access to an ISP's customers' details; disclosure of credit card slips; unauthorized access to subscribers' account data both through unauthorized disclosure and through coding errors on a website.

The guidance also provides appropriate safeguards, including encryption with a sufficiently strong and secret key; the secure storage of passwords; vulnerability scanning to diminish the risk of hacking and other breaches; regular back-ups; systems and process design to reduce the risk of breach or to mitigate its effects, such as dissociating medical information from patients' names; limiting access, and restricting access to databases to a 'need to know' and 'least privilege' basis, including reducing access provided to vendors for system maintenance.

Spyware is software—often hidden within an email attachment—that secretly harvests data within a device about its user, or applications made by the device. These are passed on to another party. The data may include the user's browsing history, log individual keystrokes (to obtain passwords), monitor user behaviour for consumer marketing purposes (so-called 'adware'), or observe the use of copyrighted works. 'Phishing' normally takes the form of an email message that appears to emanate from a trusted institution such as a bank. It seeks to entice the addressee into divulging sensitive data such as a password or credit card details. The messages are normally highly implausible—replete with spelling mistakes and other obvious defects—yet this manifest deceit manages to dupe an extraordinarily high number of recipients.

Some malware filches personal data or transforms your computer into a 'bot'—one which is remotely controlled by a third party. A 'bot' may be employed to collect email addresses, send spam, or mount attacks on corporate websites. Another form of attack is 'Denial of Service' (DoS), which uses a swarm of 'bots' or 'zombies' to inundate company websites with bogus data requests. A 'zombie' creates numerous processors dotted around the Internet under central or timed control (hence 'zombies'). An attack will pursue a website until it has been taken offline. This may endure for several days, incurring considerable costs to the victim company. They are typically accompanied by demands for money.

A new threat is 'armoured' malware. The 'armour' is an added sheath of code around the virus that allows it to enter and operate unseen. The code renders the virus invisible either by appearing to be gibberish to the computer's operating system computer or through concealing the virus by placing it elsewhere on the system. Software is now available that acts as a malware factory. It produces one unique item of malware every second. Once released, the virus is protected by built-in encryption and additional 'armoured' code.

Bugs are errors in software—particularly found in Microsoft Windows software—that may render the user's system vulnerable to attack by so-called 'crackers'. Microsoft normally responds by issuing a patch for downloading—until the next bug materializes. An 'exploit' is an attack on a particular vulnerability. Standard techniques are supported by established guidelines and programming code that circulate on the Internet.

Surveillance

The leaks by Edward Snowden, discussed earlier, exposed the prodigious scale of state surveillance conducted through the NSA's

PRISM and other programmes. Although the degree of surveillance conducted in EU countries does not appear to reach the scale seen in the US, there is little room for complacency. It was reported in early 2009 that police in the EU have been encouraged to expand the implementation of a rarely used power of intrusion—without warrant. This will permit police across Europe to hack into private computers when an officer believes that such a 'remote search' is proportionate and necessary to prevent or detect serious crime (one which attracts a prison sentence of more than three years). This could be achieved in a number of ways, including the attachment of a virus to an email message that, if opened, would covertly activate the remote search facility.

In addition, an EU directive requires telecommunications operators and ISPs to retain records of users' calls and online activity for two years in order to facilitate security services' checks on 'metadata', such as who has been communicating with whom, from where, when, and for how long. The actual content of the messages may not be read.

This directive was struck down by the European Court of Justice on the ground that it violated rights to respect for private life and the protection of personal data, adding that the use of the data without an individual's knowledge 'is likely to generate in the persons concerned a feeling that their private lives are the subject of constant surveillance.' Whether this judgment survives the security concerns of many European countries remains to be seen.

In Britain a draft Communications Data Bill failed to reach the statute book, thanks to opposition by the Liberal Democrats in the House of Commons. The proposed law would require ISPs and mobile telephone companies to maintain records (but not the content) of users' Internet browsing (including on social media), email correspondence, voice calls, Internet gaming, and mobile phone messaging services, and to store the records for twelve months. Retention of email and telephone contact data for this time is already required. Further legislation in this field is inevitable.

Cookies

These are data that the website servers transmit to a visitor's browser and are stored on his or her computer. They enable the website to recognize the visitor's computer as one with which it has previously interacted, and to remember details of the earlier transaction, including search words, and the amount of time spent reading certain pages. In other words, cookie technology enables a website—by default—furtively to put its own identifier into my PC, permanently, in order track my online conduct.

And cookies can endure; they may show an extensive list of each website visited during a particular period. Moreover, the text of the cookie file may reveal personal data previously provided. Websites such as Amazon.com justify this practice by claiming that it assists and improves the shopping experience by informing customers of books which, on the basis of their browsing behaviour, they might otherwise neglect to buy. But this gives rise to the obvious danger that my identity may be misrepresented by a concentration on tangential segments of my surfing or, on the other hand, personal data harvested from a variety of sources may be assembled to create a comprehensive lifestyle profile. I return to this subject in Chapter 5.

Hacking

Hackers were once regarded as innocuous 'cyber-snoops' who adhered to a slightly self-indulgent, but quasi-ethical, code dictating that one ought not to purloin data, but merely to report holes in the victim's system. They were, as Lessig puts it, 'a bit more invasive than a security guard, who checks office doors to make sure they are locked . . . (He) not only checked the locks but let himself in, took a quick peek around, and left a cute (or sarcastic) note saying, in effect, "Hey, stupid, you left your door open."'

While this laid-back culture eventually attracted the interest of law-enforcement authorities—who secured legislation against it—the practice continues to produce headaches. According to Simon Church of VeriSign, the online auction sites that criminals use to sell user details are merely the beginning. He anticipates that 'mashup' sites that combine different databases could be converted to criminal use. 'Imagine if a hacker put together information he'd harvested from a travel company's database with Google Maps. He could provide a tech-savvy burglar with the driving directions of how to get to your empty house the minute you go on holiday.'

Identity theft

The appropriation of an individual's personal information to commit fraud or to impersonate him or her is an escalating problem costing billions of dollars a year. In 2007 a survey by the US Federal Trade Commission found that in 2005 a total of 3.7 per cent of survey participants indicated that they had been victims of identity theft. This result suggests that approximately 8.3 million Americans suffered some form of identity theft in that year, and 10 per cent of all victims reported out-of-pocket expenses of $1,200 or more. The same percentage spent at least fifty-five hours resolving their problems. The top 5 per cent of victims spent at least 130 hours. The estimate of total losses from identity theft in the 2006 survey amounted to $15.6 billion.

The practice normally involves at least three persons: the victim, the impostor, and a credit institution that establishes a new account for the impostor in the victim's name. This may include a credit card, a utilities service, or even a mortgage.

Identity theft assumes a number of forms. Potentially the most harmful comprise credit card fraud (in which an account number is stolen in order to make unauthorized charges), new account fraud (where the impostor initiates an account or 'tradeline' in the victim's name—the offence may be undiscovered until the victim applies for credit), identity cloning (where the impostor masquerades as the victim), and criminal identity theft (in which the impostor, masquerading as the victim, is arrested for some offence, or is fined for a violation of the law).

Part of the responsibility must be laid at the door of the financial services industry itself. Their lax security methods in granting credit and facilitating electronic payment subordinates security to convenience.

DNA databases

The growing use of DNA evidence in the detection of crime has generated a need for a database of samples to determine whether an individual's profile matches that of a suspect (see Figure 3). The DNA database in England and Wales (with its 5.3 million profiles, representing 9 per cent of the population) may be the largest anywhere. It includes DNA samples and fingerprints of almost a million suspects who are never prosecuted or who are subsequently acquitted. It is hardly surprising that innocent persons should feel aggrieved by the retention of their genetic information: the potential for misuse is not a trivial matter. This dismal prospect led two such individuals to request that their profiles be expunged following their walking free. Unable to convince the English courts, they appealed to the European Court of Human Rights, which, at the end of 2008, unanimously decided that Article 8 ('respect for private life') had been violated.

Other jurisdictions tend to destroy a DNA profile when a suspect is acquitted. In Norway and Germany, for example, a sample may be kept permanently only with the approval of a court. In Sweden, only the profiles of convicted offenders who have served custodial sentences of more than two years may be retained. The US

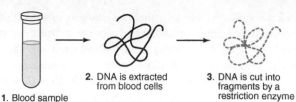

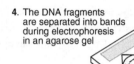

1. Blood sample

2. DNA is extracted from blood cells

3. DNA is cut into fragments by a restriction enzyme

4. The DNA fragments are separated into bands during electrophoresis in an agarose gel

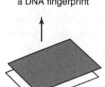

11. The X-ray film is developed to make visible the pattern of bands which is known as a DNA fingerprint

5. The DNA band pattern in the gel is transferred to a nylon membrane by a technique known as southern blotting

10. X-ray film is placed next to the membrane to detect the radioactive pattern

6. The radioactive DNA probe is prepared

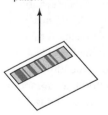

9. At this stage the radioactive probe is bound to the DNA pattern on the membrane

8. Excess DNA probe is washed off

7. The DNA probe binds to specific DNA sequences on the membrane

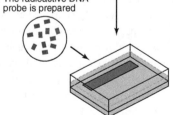

3. **The process of obtaining DNA.**

Privacy

permits the FBI to take DNA samples on arrest, but they can be destroyed on request should no charges be laid or if the suspect is acquitted. Among the 40 or so states that have DNA databases, only California permits permanent storage of profiles of individuals charged but then cleared. It has been suggested that, to avoid discrimination against certain sectors of the population (such as black males), everybody's DNA should be collected and held in the database. This drastic proposal is unlikely to attract general support. What is clear, however, is that to maintain the integrity of the system and protect privacy, the vulnerability of such sensitive genetic data requires stringent regulation.

RFID

The technology of radio frequency identification emerged as a means of inventory control to replace barcodes. An RFID system consists of three elements: a minuscule chip on each consumer item (an RFID tag) that stores a unique product identifier; an RFID reader; and a computer system attached to the reader having access to an inventory control database. The database contains extensive product information, including the contents, origin, and manufacturing history of the product. Assigning a tag to a product also discloses its location, rate, and place of sale, and, in the case of transport companies, its progress. It has applications in recalling faulty or dangerous merchandise, tracing stolen property, preventing counterfeit, and providing an audit trail to thwart corruption.

The potential of RFID is huge, and it is increasingly being used for 'contactless' payment cards, passports, and the monitoring of luggage, library books, and pets. There is no reason why humans could not be microchipped—like our dogs. It could assist the identification of Alzheimer's patients who go astray. Combining RFID and wireless fidelity networks (Wi-Fi) could facilitate real-time tracking of objects or people inside a wireless network, such as a hospital. The privacy concern is that the acceptance of these benign applications may initiate less benevolent uses; there are likely to be calls for sex offenders, prisoners, illegal immigrants, and other 'undesirables' to be tagged (see Figure 4).

There is also the fear that if RFID data were to be aggregated with other data (for example, information stored in credit or loyalty cards)—to match product data with personal information—this could allow comprehensive personal profiles of consumers to be assembled. Moreover, an increase in the use of RFID in public places, homes, and businesses, could portend an enlargement of the surveillance society. For example, let's say that my car has had an RFID affixed to the windscreen that automatically deducts any road tolls directly from my bank account, the fact that it has just passed through the toll station at Pisa may be useful to a party interested in my movements. There is plainly a need for sophisticated privacy-enhancing technologies (PETs) here.

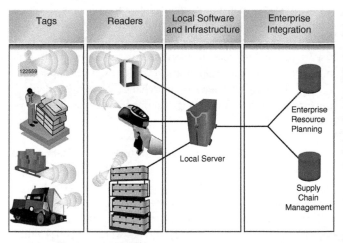

4. The escalating use of RFID technology poses numerous threats to privacy.

Global positioning system

Satellite signals are used by global positioning systems (GPSs) to establish a location. GPS chips are now common in vehicle navigation systems and mobile phones. It is possible to augment the data generated from a GPS by their assimilation into databases and aggregation with other information to create geographic information systems (GIS). In order to make or receive calls, mobile phones communicate their location to a base station. In effect, therefore, they broadcast the user's location every few minutes.

Services such as Loki use wireless signals to triangulate a position, which allows a user to obtain local weather reports, find nearby restaurants, cinemas, or shops, or share their location with friends. According to its website, 'as you travel around, MyLoki can automatically let your friends know where you are using your favourite platform—Facebook, RSS Feeds, or badges for your blog or even Twitter'. It claims to protect privacy by refraining from the collection of any personal information.

Drones

Domestic drones are increasingly being deployed in the US for surveillance. A number of American states have established legislation regulating their use. Privacy advocates have urged Congress to limit the use of drones to situations where a warrant has been acquired; in cases of an emergency; or where there are reasonable grounds to believe that the evidence collected directly relates to a specific criminal act. Images, it is argued, should then be retained only when there is reasonable suspicion that they contain evidence of a crime or where they are relevant to an ongoing investigation or trial. Recently the Governor of Washington State vetoed a bill that would have regulated the use of drones by government and police, stating that it did not go far enough to protect privacy rights. Instead, he called for a fifteen-month moratorium on purchasing or using unmanned aircraft by state agencies for anything other than emergencies such as forest fires. The original proposal to regulate drone use had broad, bipartisan support in the legislature, as well as the backing of the American Civil Liberties Union (ACLU), but Governor Inslee insisted, 'I'm very concerned about the effect of this new technology on our citizens' right to privacy. People have a desire not to see drones parked outside their kitchen window by any public agency.'

Genetic information

The ability to explore our genetic structure poses a number of privacy problems, not least the extent to which a doctor's duty to preserve patient confidentiality, enshrined in the Hippocratic Oath, adequately safeguards this sensitive information against disclosure. It raises too the intractable problem of the subject's blood relatives—and even partners and spouses—whose interest in learning the data is far from trivial.

The challenges posed by these—and other—intrusions cannot be underestimated. How have we arrived at this situation? The next chapter attempts to provide an answer.

Repelling the attacks

PETs seek to protect privacy by eliminating or reducing personal data or by preventing unnecessary or undesired processing of personal data through the use of privacy-invading technologies (PITs) without compromising the operation of the data system. Originally they took the form of 'pseudonymization tools': software that allows individuals to withhold their true identity from operating electronic systems, and to only reveal it when absolutely essential. These technologies help to reduce the amount of data collected about an individual. Their efficacy, however, depends largely on the integrity of those who have the power to revoke or nullify the shield of the pseudonym. Unhappily, governments cannot always be trusted.

Instead of pseudonymity, stronger PETs afford the tougher armour of anonymity, which prevents governments and corporations from linking data with an identified individual. This is normally achieved by a succession of intermediary-operated services. Each intermediary knows the identities of the intermediaries next to it in the chain, but has insufficient information to facilitate the identification of the previous and succeeding intermediaries. It cannot trace the communication to the originator, or forward it to the eventual recipient.

These PETs include anonymous remailers, web-surfing measures, and David Chaum's payer-anonymous electronic cash (e-cash) or 'Digicash'. The latter employs a blinding technique that sends randomly encrypted data to my bank, which then validates them (through the use of some sort of digital money) and returns the data to my hard disk. Only a serial number is provided: the recipient does not know (and does not need to know) the source of the payment. This process affords an even more powerful safeguard of anonymity. It has considerable potential in electronic copyright management systems (ECMS) with projects such as CITED (Copyright in Transmitted Electronic Documents) and COPICAT, being developed by the European Commission ESPIRIT programme. Full texts of copyrighted works are being downloaded and marketed without the owner's consent or royalty being paid. These projects seek technological solutions by which users could be charged for their use of such material. This 'tracking' of users poses an obvious privacy danger: my reading, listening, or viewing habits may be stored, and access to them obtained, for potentially sinister or harmful purposes. Blind signatures seem to be a relatively simple means by which to anonymize users.

'Do Not Track' (DNT) is a technology and policy proposal that permits users to opt out of tracking by websites that they do not visit, including advertising networks and social platforms. Microsoft, Apple, Google, and Mozilla have implemented the system on their browsers, but they are neither comprehensive nor user-friendly. And the system is, at present, self-regulatory and unenforceable.

Anonymity is an important democratic value. Even in a pre-electronic age, it facilitated participation in the political process which an individual may otherwise wish to spurn. Indeed, the US Supreme Court has held that the First Amendment protects the right to anonymous speech. There are numerous reasons why I may wish to conceal my identity behind a pseudonym or achieve anonymity in some other way. On the Internet, I may want to be openly anonymous but conduct a conversation (with either known or anonymous identities) using an anonymous remailer. I may even wish no one to know the identity of the recipient of my email. And I may not want anyone to know to which newsgroups I belong or which websites I have visited.

There are, moreover, obvious personal and political benefits of anonymity for whistle-blowers, victims of abuse, and those requiring help of various kinds. Equally (as always?), such liberties may also shield criminal activities, though the right to anonymous speech would not extend to unlawful speech. Anonymity enjoys a unique relationship with both privacy and free speech. The opportunities for anonymity afforded by the Internet are substantial; we are probably only on the brink of discovering its potential in both spheres. It raises (somewhat disquieting) questions about the question of who we are: our very identities.

In respect of data protection (see Chapter 5) the EU's Article 29 Working Party published an 'Opinion' on anonymization techniques describing various methods that data controllers use to render data anonymous. 'Once a dataset is truly anonymized and individuals are no longer identifiable,' the opinion points out, 'European data-protection law no longer applies.' The use of strong encryption to protect the security of communications has been met by resistance (notably in the US and France) and by proposals either to prohibit encryption altogether or, through means such as public key escrow, to preserve the power to intercept messages. The battle has been joined between law enforcers and cryptographers; it is likely to be protracted, especially since 'enthusiastic' is too mild a word to describe how ordinary computer users have embraced the possibility of strong encryption—Phil Zimmerman's encryption software, PGP ('Pretty Good Privacy'), for example, may now be generated in less than five minutes and is freely available on the Internet.

Further, Yahoo recently announced measures that include a system that encrypts all information being transmitted from one Yahoo data centre to another. The technology is designed to render email and other digital information flowing through data centres unintelligible to outsiders.

Technological solutions are especially useful in concealing the identity of the individual. Weak forms of digital identities are already widely used in the form of bank account and social security numbers. They provide only limited protection, for it is a simple matter to match them with the person they represent. The advent of smart cards that generate changing pseudo-identities will facilitate genuine transactional anonymity. 'Blinding' or 'blind signatures' and 'digital signatures' will significantly enhance the protection of privacy. A digital signature is a unique 'key' which provides, if anything, stronger authentication than an individual's written signature. A public key system involves two keys, one public and the other private. The advantage of a public key system is that if you are able to decrypt the message, you know that it could only have been created by the sender.

The paramount question is: is my identity *genuinely required* for the act or transaction concerned? It is here that data-protection principles, discussed in Chapter 5, come into play.

Chapter 2
An enduring value

While much of our contemporary disquiet about privacy tends to spring from technological threats to privacy, a much broader conception of the notion is adopted by many writers on the subject. It includes, in particular, 'decisional' privacy (the right of individuals to choose: whether to abort a foetus, their use of contraception, their sexual preferences, and other similar 'private' or 'personal' decisions). This right to choose is, of course, an extremely important feature of a democratic society, and is fundamental to individual autonomy and freedom, but my own view, explained in this chapter, is that matters of decisional privacy are best treated as related to, but not central instances of, the meaning of privacy—especially in our digital age. Nonetheless, the yearning for a private realm long precedes the Brave New World of bits and bytes, of electronic surveillance, and CCTV. Indeed, anthropologists have demonstrated that there is a near-universal desire for individual and group privacy in primitive societies, and that this is reflected in appropriate social norms. Moreover, we are not alone in seeking refuge from the crowd. Animals too need privacy in this sense.

What is privacy?

At the most general level, the idea of privacy embraces the desire to be left alone, free to be ourselves—uninhibited and unconstrained by the prying of others. This extends beyond snooping and unsolicited publicity to intrusions upon the 'space' we need to make intimate, personal decisions without the intrusion of the state. Thus 'privacy' is frequently employed to describe a zone demarcated as 'private' in which, for example, a woman exercises a choice as to whether she wishes to have an abortion, or an individual is free to express his or her sexuality. Debates about privacy are therefore often entangled with contentious moral questions, including the use of contraception and the right to pornography.

In any event, it is clear that at the core of our concern to protect privacy in this general sense lies a conception of the individual's relationship with society. Once we acknowledge a separation between the public and the private domain, we assume a community in which not only does such a division make sense, but also an institutional structure that makes possible an account of this sort. In other words, to postulate the 'private' presupposes the 'public'.

Over the last century or so, participation in the public realm—in society—has undergone steady erosion. We are now more self-centred. Our post-modern psychological preoccupation with 'being in touch with' our feelings, as the sociologist Richard Sennett vividly demonstrates, devastated the prospect of a genuine political community. Paradoxically, excessive intimacy has destroyed it: 'The closer people come, the less social, the more painful, the more fratricidal their relations.'

In fact, the Greeks regarded a life spent in the privacy of 'one's own' (*idion*) as, by definition, 'idiotic'. Similarly, the Romans perceived privacy as merely a temporary refuge from the life of the *res publica*. This is well described by Hannah Arendt:

> In ancient feeling the private trait of privacy, indicated in the word itself, was all-important; it meant literally a state of being deprived of something, and even of the highest and most human of man's

capacities. A man who lived only a private life, who like the slave
was not permitted to enter the public realm, or like the barbarian
had chosen not to establish such a realm, was not fully human.

Only in the late Roman Empire can one discern the initial stages of
the recognition of privacy as a zone of intimacy. As one might expect,
ancient and primitive societies display diverse attitudes to privacy. In
his seminal study *Privacy: Studies in Social and Cultural History*,
Barrington Moore examined the state of privacy in a number of early
communities, including classical Athens, Jewish society as revealed
in the Old Testament, and ancient China. In the case of China, he
illustrates how the Confucian distinction between the separate
realms of the state (public) and the family (private), as well as early
texts on courtship, the family, and friendship, generated weak rights
to privacy. In 4th century BCE Athens, on the other hand, privacy
rights were accorded stronger protection. His conclusion is that
privacy of communication was attainable only in a complex society
with strong liberal traditions.

Our modern demarcation of public and private zones occurred as
a result of a twin movement in political and legal thought. The
emergence of the nation-state and theories of sovereignty in the
16th and 17th centuries generated the concept of a distinctly public
realm. On the other hand, the identification of a private domain
free from the encroachment of the state emerged as a response to
the claims of monarchs, and, in due course, parliaments, to an
untrammelled power to make law. In other words, the appearance
of the modern state, the regulation of social and economic activities,
and the recognition of a private realm are natural prerequisites to
this separation.

Historical evidence, however, tells only part of the story. Sociological
models powerfully express the social values that capture this
transformation. A particularly useful sociological dichotomy is the
distinction between *Gemeinschaft* and *Gesellschaft*. The former,
broadly speaking, is a community of internalized norms and

traditions regulated according to status but mediated by love, duty, and a shared understanding and purpose. *Gesellschaft*, on the other hand, is a society in which self-interested individuals compete for personal material advantage in a so-called free market.

This distinction is often expressed as the difference between community and association. The former exhibits almost no division between the public and the private, while in the latter the separation is stark: the law formally regulates that which is conceived to be public. This differentiation illuminates also the political and economic order.

The segregation of public and private spheres is also a central tenet of liberalism. Indeed, 'liberalism may be said largely to have been an argument about where the boundaries of [the] private sphere lie, according to what principles they are to be drawn, whence interference derives and how it is to be checked'. The extent to which the law might legitimately intrude upon the 'private' is a recurring theme, especially in 19th century liberal doctrine: 'One of the central goals of nineteenth-century legal thought was to create a clear separation between constitutional, criminal, and regulatory law—public law—and the law of private transactions—torts, contracts, property, and commercial law.' And the question of the limits of the criminal law in enforcing 'private morality' continues to perplex legal and moral philosophers.

More than 150 years since its publication, John Stuart Mill's 'harm principle', expounded in *On Liberty*, still provides a litmus test for most libertarian accounts of the limits of interference in the private lives of individuals. For Mill:

> the sole end for which mankind are warranted, individually or
> collectively in interfering with the liberty of action of any of their
> number, is self-protection. That the only purpose for which power

can be rightfully exercised over any member of a civilized community, against his will, is to prevent harm to others. His own good, either physical or moral, is not a sufficient warrant.

The value of privacy

A life without privacy in this general sense is inconceivable. But what purposes does privacy actually serve? In addition to its significance in liberal democratic theory, privacy stakes out a sphere for creativity, psychological well-being, and our ability to love, forge social relationships, and promote trust, intimacy, and friendship.

In his classic work, Alan Westin identifies four functions of privacy that combine the concept's individual and social dimensions. First, it engenders personal autonomy; the democratic principle of individuality is associated with the need for such autonomy—the desire to avoid manipulation or domination by others. Second, it provides the opportunity for emotional release. Privacy allows us to remove our social mask:

> On any given day a man may move through the roles of stern father, loving husband, car-pool comedian, skilled lathe operator, union steward, water-cooler flirt, and American Legion committee chairman—all psychologically different roles that he adopts as he moves from scene to scene on the individual stage...Privacy...gives individuals, from factory workers to Presidents, a chance to lay their masks aside for rest. To be always 'on' would destroy the human organism.

Third, it allows us to engage in self-evaluation—the ability to formulate and test creative and moral activities and ideas. And, fourth, privacy offers us the environment in which we can share confidences and intimacies, and engage in limited and protected communication (see Box 1).

Box 1 Surveillance makes us good

'[W]hat if we *all* behaved as if we were being watched? It would lead to a more moral way of life. Who would do something unethical or immoral or illegal if they were being watched? If their illegal money transfer was being tracked? If their blackmailing phone call was being recorded? If their stick-up at the gas station was being filmed by a dozen cameras and even their retinas identified during the robbery? If their philandering was being documented in a dozen ways?'

'I don't know. I'm imagining all that would be greatly reduced.'

'Mae, we would finally be compelled to be our best selves. And I think people would be relieved. There would be this phenomenal global sigh of relief. Finally, finally, we can be good. In a world where bad choices are no longer an option, we have no choice *but* to be good.'

Dave Eggers, *The Circle*

The dilemma of privacy

Yet privacy is not an unqualified good. Seven shortcomings may briefly be identified. First, privacy is sometimes perceived as a rather quaint, prudish Victorian value; it has, in the words of one writer, 'an air of injured gentility'. Second, and more seriously, the shroud of privacy may conceal domestic oppression, especially of women by men. Feminists claim that a significant cause of women's subjugation is their relegation to the private realm of the home and family. Moreover, while the state is disposed to control the public sphere, there is a reluctance to encroach into the private realm—frequently the site of the exploitation of and violence against women.

Third, the sanctuary of privacy may weaken the detection and apprehension of criminals and terrorists. Today, of course, threats to security occupy centre-stage. Some fear that an excessively zealous defence of privacy may hinder law-enforcement authorities in the execution of their responsibilities. Fourth, it may hamper the free flow of information, impeding transparency and candour. Fifth, privacy may obstruct business efficiency and increase costs. An undue preoccupation with privacy can undermine the collection of crucial personal information, and slow down the making of commercial decisions, thereby reducing productivity.

Sixth, certain communitarian critics regard privacy as an unduly individualistic right that should not be permitted to trump other rights or community values. Finally, a powerful case is made against privacy by those, like the American judge and jurist Richard Posner, who argue—from an economic standpoint—that withholding unflattering personal information may constitute a form of deception. This important critique warrants closer examination.

In seeking to withhold or limit the circulation of personal information, is the individual engaged in a form of deception, especially when the information depicts him or her in an unfavourable light? Posner asserts:

> To the extent that people conceal personal information in order to mislead, the economic case for according legal protection to such information is no better than that for permitting fraud in the sale of goods.

But even if one were to recognize the economic perspective, it does not follow that one would accept the assessment of the economic value of withholding personal information. Individuals may be willing to trade their interest in restricting the circulation of such information against their societal interest in its free flow. In other words, Posner has not shown, and may be unable to show, that his calculation of 'competing' interests is necessarily the correct, or even the most likely, one.

Posner also argues that transaction-cost considerations may militate against the legal protection of personal information. Where the information is discrediting and accurate, there is a social incentive to make it generally available: accurate information facilitates reliance on the individual to whom the information relates. It is therefore socially efficient to allow a society a right of access to such information rather than to permit the individual to conceal it. In the case of non-discrediting or false information, the value to the individual of concealment exceeds the value of access to it by the community. Information which is false does not advance rational decision-making and is therefore of little use.

The meaning of privacy

So far, despite my initial circumspection, I have employed the term 'privacy' promiscuously. I have used it to describe a variety of conditions or interests—from seeking refuge to the intimacy of close relations. It is hardly surprising that the notion is anything but coherent. While there is general consensus that our privacy is violated by onslaughts on the private domain—in the shape of surveillance, the interception of our communications, and the activities of the paparazzi, the waters grow ever murkier when a multitude of additional grievances are crowded under the privacy umbrella.

Unfortunately for those seeking a precise delineation of this amorphous concept, the gargantuan literature on the subject has not produced a lucid or consistent meaning of a value that provides a forum for contesting, amongst other things, the rights of women (especially in respect of abortion), the use of contraceptives, the freedom of homosexuals and lesbians, the right to read or view obscene material or pornography, and some of the problems of confidentiality generated by HIV/AIDS. Harnessing privacy in the pursuit of so many disparate, sometimes competing, political and social ideals has generated a good deal of analytical confusion.

The value of privacy as a general moral, political, or social value is undeniable, but the more the notion is stretched, the greater its ambiguity. In pursuit of clarity, it is arguable that at its heart lies a desire, probably a need, to prevent information about us being known to others without our consent. But, as already stated, there are other issues that have increasingly entered the privacy arena. This is most conspicuous in the US. The expression by the Supreme Court of 'unenumerated rights' such as privacy since its seminal decisions in *Griswold v Connecticut* and *Roe v Wade* (which supported a constitutional right to privacy in respect of contraception and abortion, respectively) has resulted in privacy being equated with the liberty of personal choice: the freedom to pursue various activities, albeit those normally taking place in a private place. In other words, the concept of privacy includes the right to control access to and use of bodies. Moreover, since laws regulating abortion and certain sex acts profoundly affect both individual privacy and government power, it may, it is suggested, be useful to recognize the category as incorporating the capacity to make personal decisions—what is called 'decisional privacy'.

Incursions into the home, office, or 'private space' have also spawned the idea of 'locational privacy'—an inelegant phrase that captures that feature of privacy invaded by assaults—overt or covert—on the personal domain.

A definition?

An acceptable definition of privacy remains frustratingly elusive. Alan Westin's ubiquitous and influential idea conceives of privacy as a claim: the 'claim of individuals, groups, or institutions to determine for themselves when, how, and to what extent information about them is communicated to others'. To regard privacy as a claim (or, the more so, as a right) not only presumes the value of privacy but also fails to define its content. It would, moreover, include the use or disclosure of *any* information about an individual. A similar criticism may be levelled at those conceptions of privacy as an 'area of life' or a psychological state.

Westin's definition has, however, exerted even greater influence in respect of its description of privacy in terms of the extent to which an individual has *control* over information about him- or herself. For control over information to be equated with privacy, an individual would have to be said to have lost privacy if he or she were prevented from exercising this control, even in cases where he or she were unable to disclose personal information. This means that the value of privacy is presumed.

Similarly, if I knowingly and voluntarily disclose personal information, I do not thereby lose privacy because I am exercising—rather than relinquishing—control. But this sense of control does not adequately describe privacy, for although I may have control over whether to disclose the information, it may be obtained by other means. And if control is meant in a stronger sense (namely that to disclose information, even voluntarily, constitutes a loss of control because I am no longer able to curtail the dissemination of the information by others), it describes the *potential* rather than the *actual* loss of privacy.

Consequently, I may not attract any interest from others and therefore my privacy would receive protection whether or not I desired it! There is a distinction between my controlling the flow of information about myself, and my being known about in fact. In order to establish whether such control actually protects my privacy, according to this argument, it is also necessary to know, for instance, whether the recipient of the information is bound by restrictive norms.

Furthermore, if privacy is regarded as an aspect of broad-spectrum control (or autonomy), it is assumed that what is at issue is my freedom to choose privacy. But, as suggested above, you may choose to abandon your privacy; the control-based definition therefore relates to the question of which choices you exercise rather than the manner in which you exercise them. It is, in other words, a definition which presupposes the value of privacy.

In view of these headaches, may the answer lie in attempting to describe the *characteristics* of privacy? Again, however, considerable disagreement exists. One view is that privacy consists of 'limited accessibility'. This generates a cluster of three related but independent components—*secrecy*: information known about an individual; *anonymity*: attention paid to an individual; and *solitude*: physical access to an individual.

A loss of privacy, as distinct from an infringement of a right to privacy, occurs, in this account, where others obtain information about an individual, pay attention to an individual, or gain access to him or her. The claimed virtues of this approach are that: first, it is neutral, facilitating an objective identification of a loss of privacy; second, it demonstrates the coherence of privacy as a value; third, it suggests the utility of the concept in legal contexts (for it identifies those occasions calling for legal protection); and fourth, it includes 'typical' invasions of privacy and excludes those issues mentioned above, which, though often thought to be privacy questions, are best regarded as moral or legal issues in their own right (relating to noise, odours, prohibition of abortion, contraception, homosexuality, and so on).

Yet even this analysis presents difficulties. In particular, to avoid presuming the value of privacy, the analysis rejects definitions that limit themselves to the *quality* of the information divulged. It therefore dismisses the view that, to constitute a part of privacy, the information concerned must be 'private' in the sense of being intimate or related to the individual's identity. If a loss of privacy occurs whenever *any* information about an individual becomes known (the secrecy component), the concept is severely diluted.

It is a distortion to describe *every* instance of the dissemination of information about an individual as a loss of privacy. To the extent, however, that privacy is a function of information or knowledge about the individual, this seems to be inescapable. In other words, in so far as the question of information about an individual is concerned, some limiting or controlling factor is required. The most acceptable factor is arguably that the information be 'personal'.

To claim that whenever an individual is the subject of attention or when access to him or her is gained, the individual necessarily loses privacy is again to divest our concern for privacy of much of its meaning. Having attention focused upon you or being subjected to uninvited intrusions upon your solitude are objectionable in their own right, but our concern for the individual's privacy in these circumstances is strongest when he or she is engaged in activities which we would normally consider private. The Peeping Tom is more likely to affront our conception of what is 'private' than someone who follows us in public.

It is sometimes argued that by protecting the values underpinning privacy (property rights, human dignity, preventing or compensating the infliction of emotional distress, and so on), moral and legal discourse concerning privacy may be dispensed with. If true, this would undercut the conceptual distinctiveness of privacy. Second, even among those who deny the derivative character of privacy, there is little agreement concerning its principal defining features.

Worse, arguments about the meaning of privacy frequently proceed from fundamentally different premises. Thus, where it is described as a 'right', the issue is not seriously joined with those who regard it as a 'condition'. The former is usually a normative statement about the need for privacy (however defined); the latter merely makes a descriptive statement about 'privacy'. Moreover, claims about the desirability of privacy tend to confuse its instrumental and inherent value; privacy is regarded by some as an end in itself, while others view it as a means by which to secure other social ends such as creativity, love, or emotional release.

Privacy and personal information

Is there a better way? Without undermining the significance of privacy as an essential value, could the answer lie in isolating the issues that give rise to individuals' claims for privacy? There is little doubt that originally the archetypal complaints in the privacy field related to what the American law calls 'public disclosure of private facts' and 'intrusion upon an individual's seclusion, solitude, or private affairs'. More recently, the collection and use of computerized personal data, metadata, and other issues associated with our digital society, have, of course, become major privacy concerns.

It seems clear that, at bottom, these questions share a concern to limit the extent to which private facts about the individual are respectively published, intruded upon, or misused. This is not to suggest that certain conditions (for instance, being alone) or certain activities (such as telephone tapping) ought not to be characterized as privacy or invasions of privacy, respectively.

In locating the problems of privacy at the level of personal information, two obvious questions arise. First, what is to be understood by 'personal'; and, second, under what circumstances is a matter to be regarded as 'personal'? Is something 'personal' by virtue simply of the claim by an individual that it is so, or are there matters that are *intrinsically* personal? To claim that my political views are personal must depend on certain norms which prohibit or curtail inquiries into, or unauthorized reports of, such views. It may, however, suffice for me to invoke the norm that I am entitled to keep my views to myself.

These norms are clearly culture-relative as well as variable. As mentioned above, anthropological evidence suggests that primitive societies have differential privacy attitudes. And it can hardly be doubted that in modern societies, conceptions of what is 'private' will fluctuate. There is certainly less diffidence in most modern communities with regard to several aspects of private life than characterized societies of even fifty years ago. Is there not a class of information that may plausibly be described as 'personal'? Normally it is objected that 'privateness' is not an attribute of the information itself; that the *same* information may be regarded as very private in one context and not so private or not private at all in another.

Naturally, Jane may be more inclined to divulge intimate facts to her analyst or to a close friend than to her employer or partner. And her objection to the disclosure of the information by a newspaper might be expected to be even stronger. But the information remains 'personal' in all three contexts. What changes is the extent to which she is prepared to permit the information to become known or to be used. It is counter-intuitive to describe the information in the first context (the analyst) as 'not private at all' or even 'not so private'. We should surely want to say that the analyst is listening to *personal* facts being discussed. Were the conversation to be surreptitiously recorded or the analyst called upon to testify in court as to a patient's homosexuality or infidelity, we would want to say that *personal information* was being recorded or disclosed. The context has manifestly changed, but it affects the degree to which it would be reasonable to expect the individual to object to the information being used or spread abroad, not the *quality* of the information itself.

Any definition of 'personal information' must therefore include both elements. It should refer both to the *quality* of the information and the *desire to control* its use. The one is, in large measure, a function of the other. In other words, the concept of 'personal information' postulated here is both descriptive and normative.

Personal information, I suggest, includes those facts, communications, or opinions which relate to the individual and which it would be reasonable to expect him or her to regard as intimate or sensitive, and therefore to want to withhold, or at least to restrict their collection, use, or circulation. 'Facts' are not, of course, confined to textual data, but they encompass a wide range of information, including images, DNA, and other genetic and biometric data such as fingerprints, face and iris images, and the ever-increasing types of information about us that technology is able to uncover and exploit.

Despite disagreement over the meaning, scope, and limits of privacy, there is little uncertainty about its significance and the threats to its preservation. Few doubt that the erosion of this fundamental value must be checked. The next chapter considers its recognition as a legal right.

Chapter 3
A legal right

Queen Victoria and Prince Albert were accomplished etchers. In 1849 the royal couple wanted copies made for their private use, and sent a number of plates of their etchings to the palace printer, Strange. Several of the impressions somehow fell into the hands of a third party, Judge, who evidently obtained them through a 'mole' employed by Strange. In turn, Strange acquired them from Judge in the honest belief that they were to be publicly exhibited with the consent of Victoria and Albert. A catalogue was produced and they set about arranging the exhibition. When he learned that royal assent was non-existent, Strange withdrew his participation from the exhibition, but decided to proceed with the printing of the catalogue. His proposal was to offer it for sale along with autographs of their regal artists.

The royal couple was not amused. The prince sought an injunction to prevent the exhibition and the intended circulation of the catalogue. It was, needless to say, granted, the court shamelessly acknowledging that 'the importance which has been attached to this case arises entirely from the exalted station of the Plaintiff...'.

Though the judgments in the case turn largely on the fact that the plates were the property of the prince, the court explicitly recognized that this afforded a wider basis upon which the law 'shelters the privacy and seclusion of thoughts and sentiments committed to writing, and desired by the author to remain not generally known'.

The American genesis

This decision was a significant factor in the legendary article that in 1890 was to give birth to the legal recognition of privacy in its own right. Written by Samuel D. Warren and Louis D. Brandeis, their commentary was published in the influential *Harvard Law Review*. A few years before, the invention of the inexpensive and portable 'snap camera' by Eastman Kodak had changed the world. Individuals could be snapped at home, at work, or at play. The beginning of the end of privacy was nigh.

The two lawyers, Warren, a Boston attorney and socialite, and Brandeis, who would be appointed to the Supreme Court in 1916, had been angered by nascent media intrusion, so-called 'yellow journalism', and consequently wrote what is widely characterized as the most influential law review article ever published. It is often thought that the catalyst for their anger was that the press had snooped on Warren's daughter's wedding. But this seems unlikely since, in 1890, she was 6 years old! The more likely source of their irritation was a series of articles in a Boston high-society gossip magazine, describing Warren's swanky dinner parties.

In any event, the celebrated article condemned the press for their effrontery (foreshadowing also the threat to privacy posed by Kodak's new-fangled contraption), and contended that the common law implicitly recognized the right to privacy. Drawing upon decisions of the English courts relating to, in particular, breach of confidence, property, copyright, and defamation, they argued that these cases were merely instances and applications of a general right to privacy. The common law, they claimed, albeit under different forms, protected an individual whose privacy was invaded by the likes of a prying journalist. In so doing, the law acknowledged the importance of the spiritual and intellectual needs of man. They famously declared:

> The intensity and complexity of life, attendant upon advancing civilization, have rendered necessary some retreat from the world, and man, under the refining influence of culture, has become more sensitive to publicity so that solitude and privacy have become more essential to the individual; but modern enterprise and invention have, through invasion upon his privacy, subjected him to mental pain and distress, far greater than could be inflicted by mere bodily injury.

The common law, they reasoned, had developed from the protection of the physical person and corporeal property to the protection of the individual's '[t]houghts, emotions and sensations'. But as a result of threats to privacy from recent inventions, business methods, and the press, the common law needed to go further. An individual's right to determine the extent to which his or her thoughts, emotions, and sensations were communicated to others was already legally protected, but only in respect of authors of literary and artistic compositions and letters who could forbid any unauthorized publication. And though English cases recognizing this right were based on arguments for the protection of property, in effect they were an acknowledgement of privacy, of 'inviolate personality'.

It was not long before the line of reasoning used in these cases was put to the test. In a 1902 court decision, the plaintiff complained that her image had been used without her consent to advertise the defendant's merchandise. She was portrayed on bags of flour with the dismal pun, 'Flour of the family'. The majority of the New York Court of Appeals rejected Warren and Brandeis's thesis, holding that the privacy argument had 'not as yet an abiding place in our jurisprudence, and…cannot now be incorporated without doing violence to settled principles of law…'. There was a minority, however, that warmed to the idea, with Gray J. declaring that the plaintiff had a right to be protected against the use of her image for the defendant's commercial advantage: 'Any other principle of decision...is as repugnant to equity as it is shocking to reason.'

The Court's decision provoked general discontent. This led to the enactment by the State of New York of a statute that rendered the unauthorized use of an individual's name or image for advertising or trade purposes unlawful. Three years later, in a case involving similar facts, the Supreme Court of Georgia adopted the reasoning of Gray J. The Warren and Brandeis argument, 15 years after its publication, had prevailed. Most American states have since incorporated the 'right to privacy' into their law. Yet, despite the authors' heavy reliance on the judgments of English courts, no comparable development has occurred in England or in other common law jurisdictions.

Over the years, the American common law maintained its steady expansion of the protection of privacy. In 1960 Dean Prosser, a leading tort expert, expounded the view that the law now recognized not one tort, 'but a complex of four different interests...tied together by the common name, but otherwise [with] nothing in common'. He delineated their nature as follows:

> The first tort consists in intruding upon the plaintiff's seclusion or solitude or into his private affairs. The wrongful act is the intentional interference with the plaintiff's solitude or seclusion. It includes the physical intrusion into the plaintiff's premises and eavesdropping (including electronic and photographic surveillance, bugging, and telephone-tapping). Three requirements must be satisfied: (a) there must be an actual prying); (b) the intrusion must offend a reasonable man; (c) it must be an intrusion into something private.

The second tort is the public disclosure of embarrassing private facts about the plaintiff. Prosser distinguished three elements of the tort:

(a) there must be publicity (to disclose the facts to a small group of people would not suffice); (b) the facts disclosed must be private facts (publicity given to matters of public record is not tortious); (c) the facts disclosed must be offensive to a reasonable man of ordinary sensibilities.

Third, he identified a tort that consists of publicity that places the plaintiff in a false light in the public eye. This is usually committed where an opinion or utterance (such as spurious books or views) is publicly attributed to the plaintiff or where his or her picture is used to illustrate a book or article with which he or she has no reasonable connection. The publicity must again be 'highly offensive to a reasonable person'.

Finally, Prosser distinguished the tort of appropriation, for the defendant's advantage, of the plaintiff's name or likeness. The advantage derived by the defendant need not be a financial one; it has, for instance, been held to arise where the plaintiff was wrongly named as father on a birth certificate. The statutory tort, which exists in several states, on the other hand, normally requires the unauthorized use of the plaintiff's identity for commercial (usually advertising) purposes. The recognition of this tort establishes what has been dubbed a 'right of publicity' under which an individual is able to decide how he or she desires to exploit his or her name or image commercially. The four forms of invasion of privacy, according to Prosser, were connected only in that each constituted an interference with the 'right to be let alone'.

This fourfold segregation of the right to privacy is regarded by some as misconceived because it undermines the Warren and Brandeis axiom of 'inviolate personality' and neglects its moral basis as an aspect of human dignity. The classification has nevertheless assumed a prominent place in American tort law, although, as predicted by one legal scholar, Harry Kalven, it has to a large extent ossified the conception into four types:

> [G]iven the legal mind's weakness for neat labels and categories
> and given the deserved Prosser prestige, it is a safe prediction that
> the fourfold view will come to dominate whatever thinking is done
> about the right of privacy in the future.

The vicissitudes of these four torts have been charted in an
immense torrent of academic and popular literature. Nor has
this development been restricted to the US. Virtually every
advanced legal system has, to a greater or lesser extent, sought to
recognize certain aspects of privacy either by its constitutional
recognition, through specific legislation, or scattered across
diverse statutes or regulations. They include Austria, Brazil,
Canada, China, Denmark, Estonia, France, Germany, Greece,
Holland, Hungary, Ireland, India, Italy, Lithuania, Mexico,
New Zealand, Norway, the Philippines, Russia, Singapore,
South Africa, South Korea, Spain, Taiwan, Thailand, and the
majority of Latin American countries.

A constitutional right

These four torts remained the effective means by which the
American law protected privacy. And they marked, more or less,
the confines of the constitutional protection of privacy as well.
The principal concern of Warren and Brandeis was, of course,
what we would now call media intrusion. Several years later,
however, Justice Brandeis (as he now was) delivered a powerful
dissent in the case of *Olmstead v United States* in 1928. He
declared that the Constitution conferred 'as against the
Government, the right to be let alone', adding, 'To protect that
right, every unjustifiable intrusion by the Government upon the
privacy of the individual, whatever the means employed, must be
deemed a violation of the Fourth Amendment.' That view was
adopted by the Supreme Court in *Katz v United States*. Since
then privacy as the right to be let alone has repeatedly been
invoked by the Supreme Court.

The most significant—and controversial—development came in 1965 with the Supreme Court's decision in *Griswold v Connecticut*. It declared unconstitutional a Connecticut statute prohibiting the use of contraceptives—because it violated the right of marital privacy, a right 'older than the Bill of Rights'. The Constitution makes no mention of the right of privacy. Yet in a series of cases the Supreme Court has—via the Bill of Rights (particularly the First, Third, Fourth, Fifth, and Ninth Amendments)—recognized, amongst other privacy rights, that of 'associational privacy', 'political privacy', and 'privacy of counsel'. It has also set the limits of protection against eavesdropping and unlawful searches.

By far the most divisive 'privacy' decision that the Court has decided is the case of *Roe v Wade* in 1973. It held, by a majority, that the abortion law of Texas was unconstitutional as it represented a violation of the right to privacy. Under that law, abortion was criminalized, except when performed to save the pregnant woman's life. The Court held that states may prohibit abortion to protect the life of the foetus only in the third trimester. The judgment, which has been described as 'undoubtedly the best-known case the US Supreme Court has ever decided', is concurrently welcomed by feminists and deplored by many Christians (see Figure 5). It is the slender thread by which the right of American women to a lawful abortion hangs. There appears to be no middle ground. The jurist, Ronald Dworkin, forthrightly depicts the intensity of the skirmish:

> The war between anti-abortion groups and their opponents is America's new version of the terrible seventeenth-century European civil wars of religion. Opposing armies march down streets or pack themselves into protests at abortion clinics, courthouses, and the White House, screaming at and spitting on and loathing one another. Abortion is tearing America apart.

Another 'privacy' judgment of the Court that generated a hullabaloo was *Bowers v Hardwick* in 1986, in which a bare

5. The US Supreme Court's decision of *Roe v Wade* in 1973 sparked a controversy that persists to this day.

majority held that the privacy protections of the due process clause did not extend to homosexual acts between consenting adults in private: 'No connection between family, marriage, or procreation on the one hand and homosexual conduct on the other has been demonstrated.'

This decision was explicitly overruled in *Lawrence v Texas* in which, by a majority of six to three, the Supreme Court decided that it had construed the liberty interest too narrowly. The majority held that substantive due process under the Fourteenth Amendment entailed the freedom to engage in intimate consensual sexual conduct. Its effect is to nullify all legislation throughout the US that purports to criminalize sodomy between consenting same-sex adults in private.

The American experience is both influential and instructive. Other common law jurisdictions continue to wrestle with the intractable problems of definition, scope, and reconciling privacy with other rights, especially freedom of expression. It is fair to say, as a generalization, that the common law is interest-based, while the continental tradition of civil law jurisdictions tends to be rights-based. In other words, while the English law, for example, adopts a pragmatic case-by-case approach to the protection of privacy, French law conceives of privacy as a fundamental human right. This disparity has nevertheless been attenuated by the impact of the European Convention on Human Rights (ECHR) and other declarations and directives emanating from Brussels, and from judgments of the European Court of Human Rights in Strasbourg. The intensity of this side-wind is most conspicuously evident in the adoption by the UK of the ECHR by the Human Rights Act of 1998, as will become clear later in this chapter.

Common law advances

It is not only the law of England and Wales that still grapples with the predicament of privacy. Australia, New Zealand, Ireland,

Canada, Hong Kong, and other common law jurisdictions continue to do so. The English law, despite several commissions, committees, and attempts at legislation, remains uncertain and ambiguous. In 1972 the Younger Committee rejected the idea of a general right of privacy created by statute. It concluded that it would burden the court 'with controversial questions of a social and political character', arguing that judges would be likely to encounter problems balancing privacy with competing interests such as freedom of expression. The committee recommended the creation of a new crime and tort of unlawful surveillance, a new tort of disclosure or other use of information unlawfully acquired, and the consideration of the law on breach of confidence (which protects confidential information entrusted by one party to another) as a possible means by which privacy could be safeguarded. Similar reports have been produced in other common law jurisdictions.

In recent years a spate of celebrity litigation has presented the courts with an opportunity to examine whether, in the absence of explicit common law privacy protection, the remedy of breach of confidence might provide a makeshift solution. These are best considered in Chapter 4. They demonstrate how a right of privacy is slouching towards the highest court to be born. One such case involved the publication of photographs taken surreptitiously of the wedding of movie stars Michael Douglas and Catherine Zeta-Jones, and is also discussed in Chapter 4. Lord Hoffmann declared in the House of Lords (now the Supreme Court) that the:

> coming into force of the Human Rights Act 1998 weakens the argument for saying that a general tort of invasion of privacy is needed to fill gaps in the existing remedies. Sections 6 and 7 of the Act are in themselves substantial gap fillers; if it is indeed the case that a person's rights under Article 8 have been infringed by a public authority, he will have a statutory remedy. The creation of a general tort will...pre-empt the controversial question of the extent, if any, to which the Convention requires the state to provide

remedies for invasions of privacy by persons who are not public authorities.

The impact of this Act (which incorporates into English law Article 8 of the ECHR) cannot be overstated. It provides for the protection of the right to respect for family life, home, and correspondence. This measure, at least in the mind of one senior judge, gives 'the final impetus to the recognition of a right of privacy in English law'. Though his conviction may not be shared by all members of the judiciary, the analysis of privacy exhibited in recent cases suggests that the effect of Article 8 is to supply, at least, the potential for the horizontal application of the rights in this Article. In fact, recent decisions explicitly acknowledge the existence of a new privacy tort under the sway of Article 8. It should be noted, however, that this Article does not protect 'privacy' *stricto sensu*. In fact, if it protects 'privacy' at all, it protects the right to *'respect'* for privacy. From a legal standpoint, its purview is agonizingly large. The European Court of Human Rights has construed it to include 'physical and psychological integrity', protection of one's environment, identity, and personal autonomy. This conceptual indeterminacy resembles the exasperating imprecision of Warren and Brandeis's 'right to be let alone'. The protection of the 'right to respect for…private and family life, [and]…home' plainly opens the door to an alarming range of activities.

As in Britain, deliberations about the need for legal protection have preoccupied law-reform commissions at both state and federal level in Australia. In 2014 the Australian Law Reform Commission published a discussion paper on the introduction of a statutory cause of action for serious invasions of privacy. Nor have their courts been idle. In a significant decision in 2001, a majority at the High Court of Australia tilted gingerly towards the recognition of a privacy tort. In *Australian Broadcasting Corporation v Lenah Game Meats Pty Ltd*, the Court, acknowledging the inadequacy of Australian law, expressed its support for the judicial development in common law jurisdictions of a common law action for invasion of privacy. In specifying what might constitute an unwarranted invasion of privacy, the Court stated:

> Certain kinds of information about a person, such as information relating to health, personal relationships, or finances, may be easy to identify as private; as may certain kinds of activity, which a reasonable person, applying contemporary standards of morals and behaviour, would understand to be meant to be unobserved. The requirement that disclosure or observation of information or conduct would be highly offensive to a reasonable person of ordinary sensibilities is in many circumstances a useful practical test of what is private.

The decision, though inconclusive on the central issue, does suggest that the High Court, when presented with a more deserving plaintiff (this one was an abattoir whose cruel practices the Australian Broadcasting Corporation wished to expose), may recognize that a privacy tort may not be entirely unthinkable.

In 2005 the New Zealand Court of Appeal took a significant step towards recognizing a common law tort of privacy. In the case of *Hosking v Runting*, the defendants took pictures of the plaintiffs' 18-month-old twin daughters in the street, being pushed in their buggy by their mother. The father is a well-known television personality. The couple sought an injunction to prevent publication. The trial court held that New Zealand law did not recognize a cause of action in privacy based on the public disclosure of photographs taken in a public place. But, though the Court of Appeal dismissed the plaintiffs' appeal, it decided (by a three to two majority) that a case had been made out for a remedy for 'breach of privacy by giving publicity to private and personal information'. This view was based principally upon its interpretation of the English courts' analysis of the remedy for breach of confidence, as well as the fact that it was consistent with New Zealand's obligations under the International Covenant on Civil and Political Rights (ICCPR) and the United Nations' Convention on the Rights of the Child. The court also considered that their judgment facilitated the reconciliation of competing values, and enabled New Zealand to draw upon the extensive experience of the US.

In their judgments, Gault P and Blanchard J specified two essential requirements for a claim to succeed. First, the plaintiff must have a reasonable expectation of privacy; and, second, there must be publicity given to private facts that would be considered highly offensive to an objective reasonable person.

The Privacy Act of 1993 provides that any person may complain to the Privacy Commissioner alleging that any action is or appears to be 'an interference with the privacy of an individual'. If the Privacy Commissioner finds that the complaint has substance, he or she may refer it to the Proceedings Commissioner appointed under the Human Rights Act 1993, who may in turn bring proceedings in the Complaints Review Tribunal. The Tribunal may make an order prohibiting a repetition of the action complained of or requiring the interference to be rectified. It has the power to award damages.

While Ireland does not explicitly recognize a general right to privacy at common law, the courts have fashioned a constitutional right to privacy out of Article 40.3.1 of the Constitution under which the State guarantees to respect, defend, and vindicate the personal rights of the citizen. So, for example, in 1974 the majority of the Supreme Court held that privacy was included among these rights. Succeeding judgments have indicated that the Article extends to some invasions of privacy by interception of communications and surveillance.

Other approaches

The continental attitude to privacy is based on the concept of the 'right of personality'. In Germany this right is guaranteed by the Basic Law. Article 1 imposes on all state authorities a duty to respect and protect 'the dignity of man'. Article 2(1) provides that 'Everyone shall have the right to the free development of his personality in so far as he does not violate the rights of others or offend against the constitutional order or the moral code.' These two articles combine to establish a general right to one's own personality; and the right to respect for one's private sphere of life is an emanation of this personality right.

In addition, the courts protect privacy as part of the right of personality under the Civil Code. They also employ the law of delict to provide a remedy against conduct injurious to human dignity such as the unauthorized publication of the intimate details of a person's private life; the right not to publish medical reports without the patient's consent; the right not to have one's conversation recorded without one's knowledge and consent; the right not to have one's private correspondence opened—whether or not it is actually read; the right not to be photographed without consent; the right to a fair description of one's life; and the right not to have personal information misused by the press.

The German courts recognize three spheres of personality: the 'intimate', the 'private', and the 'individual'. The 'intimate sphere' covers one's thoughts and feelings and their expression, medical information, and sexual behaviour. Given its particularly private nature, this species of information enjoys absolute protection. The 'private sphere' includes information which, while neither intimate nor secret (such as facts about one's family and home life), is nevertheless private and therefore attracts qualified protection—disclosure might be justified in the public interest. The 'individual sphere' relates to an individual's public, economic, and professional life, one's social and occupational relations. It attracts the lowest degree of protection.

Privacy is zealously protected in France. Though it is not explicitly mentioned in the French Constitution, the Constitutional Council in 1995 extended the concept of 'individual freedom' in Article 66 to the right to privacy. Privacy was thus elevated to a constitutional right. In addition, Article 9 of the French Civil Code provides that 'Everyone has the right to respect for his private life…'. This has been interpreted by the courts to include a person's identity (name, date of birth, religion, address, and so on) and information about a person's health, matrimonial situation, family, sexual relationships, sexual orientation, and his or her way of life in general. It is also a criminal offence to encroach intentionally upon a private place by taking a photograph or by making a recording. Damages may be awarded for violations.

There has been a recent shift in the media's policy in regard to reporting on the private lives of politicians, not excluding that of a president (see Figure 6). In 2014 the actress Julie Gayet was awarded 15,000 Euros in damages against the French magazine, *Closer*, after it published images which supported its claim that President Hollande was engaged in affair with Miss Gayet. It published photographs of him leaving her apartment following a romantic assignation. Earlier, the President's former partner, First Lady Valérie Trierweiler, succeeded in her action against the same magazine, after it published images taken while she was on holiday in Mauritius. In a later decision the photographer was sentenced to a suspended fine of 1,000 Euros for snapping her at the wheel of a car.

The Italian Constitution protects the right to privacy as representing a constituent of an individual's personality. Privacy as such is not specifically mentioned, but various sections of the document combine to protect the inviolability of the home; this section is connected to the Criminal Code's provisions on searches,

6. The French President's romantic life vividly depicted in celebrity magazines.

and the protection of correspondence and communications. An invasion of privacy may give rise to a claim under the Civil Code, which provides that a person who intentionally or negligently commits an act that causes unreasonable harm to another is liable to compensate the latter. The Civil Code declares also that the publication of a person's image may be restrained if it causes prejudice to his or her dignity or reputation.

Article 10 of the Dutch Constitution guarantees the right to privacy, but it is a right subject to qualification; though the Supreme Court has held that the right to freedom of speech does not excuse an infringement of privacy, it will consider all circumstances in a privacy action, allowing a defendant journalist the possibility to demonstrate that the publication in question was reasonable. Article 1401 of the Civil Code imposes a general liability for causing wrongful harm to others; it has been interpreted to include harm caused by publishing injurious private information without justification. The criminal law punishes the trespassing of a person's home, eavesdropping on private conversations, and unauthorized taking of photographs of individuals on private property and subsequent publication of any photographs so acquired.

While neither the Canadian Constitution nor its Charter of Rights and Freedoms include an explicit reference to privacy, the courts have filled the gap by construing the right to be secure against unreasonable search or seizure (Section 8 of the Charter) as embodying an individual's right to expect a reasonable level of privacy. There is no common law right of privacy along American lines, but the lower courts have shown a willingness to stretch existing causes of action, such as trespass or nuisance, to protect the privacy of a victim. The common law deficiency has been resolved in a number of Canadian provinces by the enactment of a statutory tort of invasion of privacy. In British Columbia, Manitoba, Newfoundland, and Saskatchewan the tort of 'violation of privacy' is actionable without proof of damage. The precise formulation of the tort differs in each province.

Quebec, as a civil law jurisdiction, has developed its remedy through the interpretation of general provisions of civil liability in the former Civil Code. The present protection, however, is explicitly incorporated in the new Civil Code. It provides that every person has a right to the respect of his or her reputation and privacy, and that no one may invade the privacy of another person except with the consent of that person or his or her heirs, or unless it has been authorized by law. The forms of privacy-invading conduct specified cover a fairly wide range of conduct. In addition, Section 5 of the Quebec Charter of Human Rights and Freedoms declares that every person has a right to respect for his or her private life. This provision is directly enforceable between citizens. The 1994 Uniform Privacy Act clarifies and augments the existing provincial statutes.

The international dimension

A fairly generous right to privacy is an acknowledged human right, and is recognized in most international instruments. So, for example, Article 12 of the United Nations Declaration of Human Rights and Article 17 of the ICCPR both provide that:

(1) No one shall be subjected to arbitrary or unlawful interference with his privacy, family, home or correspondence, nor to unlawful attacks on his honour and reputation.

(2) Everyone has the right to the protection of the law against such interference or attacks.

Article 8 of the ECHR declares,

(1) Everyone has the right to respect for his private and family life, his home and his correspondence.

(2) There shall be no interference by a public authority with the exercise of this right except such as is in accordance with the law and is necessary in a democratic society in the interests of national security, public safety or the economic well-being of the country, for the prevention of disorder or crime, for the protection of health or morals, or for the protection of the rights and freedoms of others.

The European Court of Human Rights in Strasbourg has had its hands fairly full adjudicating complaints from individuals seeking redress for alleged infractions of Article 8. Their grievances have exposed deficiencies in the domestic law of several European jurisdictions. For example, in *Gaskin v United Kingdom*, the Court held that the right to respect for private and family life imposed a duty to provide an individual with personal information about him- or herself held by a public authority. However, in *Leander v Sweden*, the Court ruled that such access could legitimately be denied to an applicant where the information related to national security, for example for the purpose of vetting an individual for a sensitive position, provided there is a satisfactory process by which the decision not to provide the information may be reviewed. Two of the Court's leading decisions in regard to telephone-tapping are discussed below. Some of its important judgments regarding media intrusion are considered in Chapter 4.

Intrusion

Modern spies no longer rely on unaided eyes and ears. As discussed in Chapter 1, an array of electronic devices renders their task relatively simple. And, in the face of these technological advances, the traditional physical or legal means of protection are unlikely to prove particularly effective; the former because radar and laser beams are no respecters of walls or windows; the latter because, in the absence of an encroachment upon the individual's property, the law of trespass will not assist the beleaguered victim of electronic surveillance. The interest protected is the plaintiff's property rather than his or her privacy.

Physical intrusions into private premises raise similar questions to those generated by the interception of private conversations and correspondence, electronic or otherwise. No civilized society can permit the unauthorized entry and search of a person's home without a valid warrant issued in advance, normally by a court. The prevention, detection, and prosecution of criminal conduct frequently require searches of private premises by the police and other law enforcement authorities. This is a matter that raises deeper questions of policy that extend beyond the protection of privacy. It is nevertheless clear, especially in a modern industrialized society, that electronic surveillance, interception of correspondence, and telephone-tapping call for systematic and fairly elaborate legislative machinery to control, in particular, the circumstances under which the law will permit the use of such devices, and their legitimate application in the pursuit of offenders and the administration of criminal justice.

The laws of many democratic countries regulate the exercise of covert surveillance by a judicial authority. Normally a court order sets out the restrictions, including time limits, on the exercise of this power which is especially pernicious since it involves monitoring not only what the subject says, but also those to whom he or she speaks. Most are likely to be wholly innocent interlocutors.

Surveillance and terrorism

The magnitude of the NSA's surveillance operations, as revealed by whistleblower, Edward Snowden, was described in Chapter 1, but more conventional means of spying continue to be employed. A powerful weapon in the so-called 'war on terror' is the wiretap. Its use has predictably intensified since the attacks of 11 September 2001. Within six weeks of this date, the US Congress had enacted the United and Strengthening America by Providing Appropriate Tools Required to Intercept and Obstruct Terrorism Act (USA PATRIOT Act). This is merely one of several measures that have been introduced to authorize the surveillance of a wide range of activities, including telephone calls, email, and Internet communications, by a number of law-enforcement officials. The provisions of a series of pre-11 September statutes—such as the Wiretap Statute, the Electronic Communications Privacy Act (ECPA), and the Foreign Intelligence Surveillance Act (FISA)—have been substantially amended, significantly diminishing their privacy safeguards.

Privacy advocates and civil libertarians have condemned numerous features of this highly controversial legislation. Among their concerns is the fact that it reduces the judicial oversight of electronic surveillance by subjecting private Internet communications to a minimal standard of review. The Act also permits law-enforcement authorities to obtain what is, in effect, a 'blank warrant'; it authorizes 'scattershot' intelligence wiretap orders that do not need to specify the place to be searched or require that only the target's conversations be listened to.

Another disquieting feature of the statute is the power it affords the Federal Bureau of Investigation (FBI) to use its intelligence authority to evade judicial review of the 'probable cause' requirement of the Fourth Amendment which requires that search warrants specify the place to be searched. It prevents abuses such as random searches of the homes of innocent persons based on a warrant obtained to search someone else's home. In other words, in the case of electronic surveillance, the specificity requirement of the Fourth Amendment obliges law-enforcement officers applying for a court order to specify the telephone they wish to tap.

A solution?

There is no perfect system. But, at the very least one would expect democratic societies to regulate this highly intrusive form of surveillance in a manner that ensures that the legitimate and reasonable expectations of its citizens are respected. In deciding whether to grant an application for a warrant to carry out covert surveillance, a court ought to satisfy itself that the proposed intrusion has a legitimate purpose. It should ensure that the means of investigation are proportionate to the immediacy and gravity of the alleged offence, balancing the need for the surveillance against the intrusiveness of the activity on the subject and others who may be affected by it. There must be a reasonable suspicion that the target is involved in the commission of a serious crime. It should also be clear that information relevant to the purpose of the surveillance is likely to be acquired, and that such information cannot reasonably be obtained by less intrusive means.

In reaching its decision, one would be entitled to assume that a judicial officer would have regard to the immediacy and gravity of the serious crime or the threat to public security, the place where the intrusion will occur, the method of intrusion to be employed, and the nature of any device to be used.

A court should consider the 'reasonable expectation of privacy' in the particular circumstances of the case. In respect of wiretapping, the argument is sometimes made that a telephone user's expectation of privacy may be regarded as reasonable in cases where the eavesdropper turns out to be a private individual, but not in cases where it is the police acting under lawful authority. This is said to be based on an acceptance of risk, but it is difficult to see how such a distinction can be legitimately drawn. If I am entitled to assume that my private conversation will not be overheard by a private individual, why should that assumption be any less strong when the eavesdropper turns out to be the police?

A further recurring difficulty concerns the standards to be applied in the case of 'non-consensual surveillance' as opposed to 'participant monitoring'. The former occurs where a private conversation is intercepted by a person who is not party to the conversation and who has not obtained the consent of any of those who are. 'Participant monitoring', on the other hand, includes cases in which a person uses a listening device to transmit a conversation to someone who is not party to the conversation, or where a participant of a conversation records it without the consent of the other person(s). It is frequently argued that, while non-consensual surveillance ought to be legally controlled, participant monitoring—especially when used in law enforcement—is justifiable. But this neglects the distinctive interests that underpin the concern to protect the content and, perhaps even more importantly, the manner in which conversations are conducted. Moreover, though participant monitoring is a useful aid in the detection of crime, and arguably constitutes less of a risk to privacy than its non-consensual counterpart, 'the party to the conversation who secretly makes a recording can present matters in a way that is entirely favourable to his position because he controls the situation. He knows he is recording it.'

Europe

The European Court of Human Rights has been particularly energetic in this area. It is instructive briefly to compare two of its important, early decisions on the subject, one relating to Germany, the other to the UK. The telephone-tapping in *Klass v Federal Republic of Germany* complied with the German statute. In *Malone v United Kingdom*, however, it was conducted without a comprehensive legislative framework. Although both involved analogue telephones, the principles expressed are sufficiently general to apply to digital telephony, as well as to the interception of written correspondence, and perhaps also to other forms of surveillance.

German law sets out stringent restrictions on interception including the requirement that applications be made in writing, that a basis should exist in fact for suspecting a person of planning, committing, or having committed certain criminal or subversive acts, and that the surveillance should cover only the specific suspect or his or her presumed contact persons: exploratory or general surveillance is therefore not permitted. The law provides also that it must be shown that other investigatory methods would be ineffective or considerably more difficult. The interception should be supervised by a judicial officer who may reveal only information that is relevant to the inquiry; he or she is obliged to destroy any remaining information that has been collected. The relevant intercepted information must then also itself be destroyed when no longer required; it may not be used for any other purpose.

Furthermore, the law requires that an interception be immediately discontinued as soon as the requirements for it have ended, and that the subject be notified as soon as it is possible to do so without jeopardizing the purpose of the interception. The subject of the interception may then challenge the lawfulness of this interception in an administrative court, and he or she may claim damages in a civil court if prejudice is proved.

In addition, the German Basic Law protects the secrecy of all communication by email, post, and telephone. The Court therefore had to decide whether interference would be justified under Article 8(2) of the ECHR as being 'in accordance with the law' and necessary in a democratic society 'in the interests of national security... or for the prevention of disorder or crime'. While the Court acknowledged the need for legislation to protect these interests, it held that the question was not the need for such provisions, but whether they contained sufficient safeguards against abuse.

The applicants contended that the legislation violated Article 8 of the ECHR because it lacked a requirement that the subject of the interception be 'invariably' notified following the termination of the surveillance. The Court held that this was not inherently incompatible with Article 8, provided that the subject was informed after the termination of the surveillance measures as soon as notification could be made without endangering the purpose of those measures.

In *Malone v United Kingdom*, the plaintiff, who, at his trial on a number of charges relating to the handling of stolen property, on learning that his telephone conversations had been intercepted, issued a writ against the police. He argued, first, that telephone-tapping was an unlawful infringement of his rights of privacy, property, and confidentiality; second, that it contravened Article 8 of the ECHR; and, third, that the Crown had no legal authority to intercept calls since no such power had been conferred by the law. When he lost his case, he took his grievance to the European Court of Human Rights, where, not surprisingly, he was successful. The Court unanimously held that the Convention had indeed been breached. As a result, the British Government acknowledged that a statute was required, and the Interception of Communications Act of 1985 was put in place. It establishes a fairly comprehensive framework, the centrepiece of which is the provision empowering the secretary of state to issue warrants where he or she considers it necessary in the interests of national security, to prevent or detect serious crime, or safeguard economic well-being.

In a more recent case, *Kennedy v United Kingdom*, the applicant alleged that local calls to his telephone were not being put through to him and that he was receiving a number of hoax calls. He suspected that his post, telephone, and email communications were being intercepted. The Court held that the UK's Regulation of Investigatory Powers Act (RIPA) did not breach Article 8 of the ECHR. It found that the domestic law on the interception of internal communications indicated with adequate clarity the procedures for the authorization and processing of interception warrants as well as the processing, communication, and destruction of intercept material collected.

While the interception of communications obviously assists in apprehending criminals, preventing crime and terrorism, the onus is on those who wish to employ this indiscriminate method of investigation to show that there is an overwhelming need to do so, that it is likely to be effective, and that there are no acceptable alternatives. If this cannot be demonstrated, it becomes virtually impossible to justify the practice, 'not because we wish to hamper law enforcement, but because there are values we place above efficient police work'.

A prudent approach to the problem would ensure that where the surveillance materials have been acquired in a seriously unconscionable manner, such that it would gravely undermine public confidence in the administration of justice, the information obtained should not be admitted in evidence at court.

Chapter 4
Privacy and freedom of expression

Celebrities—stars of screen, radio, television, pop music, sport, and the catwalk—are regarded as fair game by the paparazzi (see Figure 7). Supermodel Naomi Campbell was photographed leaving a meeting of Narcotics Anonymous. The British tabloid newspaper the *Daily Mirror* published the pictures, together with articles claiming that she was receiving treatment for her drug addiction. She denied publicly that she was an addict, and sued the

7. The appetite for celebrity gossip fuels an increasingly sensationalist media.

newspaper for damages. The trial court and the Court of Appeal found against her. They held that by mendaciously asserting to the media that she did not take drugs, she had rendered it legitimate for the media to put the record straight. But her appeal to the House of Lords succeeded, and she was awarded compensation for a violation of her privacy.

Photographs of the wedding of Michael Douglas and Catherine Zeta-Jones were surreptitiously taken, despite explicit notice having been given to all guests forbidding 'photography or video devices at the ceremony or reception'. The couple had entered into an exclusive publication contract with *OK!* magazine, but its rival, *Hello!*, sought to publish these pictures. The stars reached for their lawyers, and won. Cases such as these raise a number of difficult questions discussed in this chapter.

Public places

What if a person is photographed in an ostensibly public place? The paparazzi frequently snap pictures of celebrities while they are shopping, eating in a restaurant, or simply walking in the street. The victims' complaint may be based on the nuisance caused by the photographer. Or it may be based on the publication of the pictures thereby obtained. Or both.

Legal approaches inevitably differ according to the jurisdiction. In the US, an individual generally loses protection in a public place (see Figure 7). Elsewhere, however, there is a growing recognition of the need to protect the privacy of individuals, especially children, in public places—particularly if the photographs taken are then published. There have been a number of recent cases involving the photographing in a public place of children of celebrities. A New Zealand court, we saw in the last chapter, was sympathetic to the claim of the celebrity parent of the 18-month-old twin daughters being pushed by their mother in their buggy in the street. And the English Court of Appeal was willing to protect the rights of the children of *Harry Potter* author J.K. Rowling who were pictured in similar conditions.

Most recently, the children of pop star, Paul Weller, obtained damages in respect of an article published online which showed photographs of him and some of his children shopping in the street and sitting in a café in Los Angeles. The Court found in favour of the children, concluding that the rights enshrined in Article 8 prevailed over those specified in Article 10 (see Box 2). It relied both on the J.K. Rowling decision, and, more importantly, on a series of cases brought in the European Court of Human Rights by Caroline Princess of Hannover which, broadly speaking, held that for the media to avoid liability it would need to demonstrate that the publication 'contributed to a debate of general interest'.

Princess Caroline of Monaco complained that paparazzi employed by several German magazines had photographed her while she was engaged in a variety of quotidian activities, including eating in a restaurant courtyard, horse riding, canoeing, playing with her children, shopping, skiing, kissing a boyfriend, playing tennis, sitting on a beach, and so on. A German court found in her favour in respect of the photographs which, although captured in a public place, were taken when she had 'sought seclusion'.

But, while accepting that some of the pictures were sufficiently intimate to warrant protection (such as those of her with her children or in the company of a boyfriend sitting in a secluded section of a restaurant courtyard), the Court dismissed her complaint in regard to the remainder of the photographs. She turned to the European Court, which acknowledged that Article 8 (see Box 2) applied, but sought to balance the protection of the princess's private life against that of freedom of expression as guaranteed by Article 10 of the Convention (again, see Box 2). Taking and publishing photographs, it decided, was a subject in which the protection of an individual's rights and reputation assumed especial significance since it did not concern the

Box 2 The European Convention on Human Rights

ARTICLE 8

Right to respect for private and family life

1. Everyone has the right to respect for his private and family life, his home and his correspondence.

2. There shall be no interference by a public authority with the exercise of this right except such as is in accordance with the law and is necessary in a democratic society in the interests of national security, public safety or the economic well-being of the country, for the prevention of disorder or crime, for the protection of health or morals, or for the protection of the rights and freedoms of others.

ARTICLE 10

Freedom of expression

1. Everyone has the right to freedom of expression. This right shall include freedom to hold opinions and to receive and impart information and ideas without interference by public authority and regardless of frontiers. This Article shall not prevent States from requiring the licensing of broadcasting, television or cinema enterprises.

2. The exercise of these freedoms, since it carries with it duties and responsibilities, may be subject to such formalities, conditions, restrictions or penalties as are prescribed by law and are necessary in a democratic society, in the interests of national security, territorial integrity or public safety, for the prevention of disorder or crime, for the protection of health or morals, for the protection of the reputation or rights of others, for preventing the disclosure of information received in confidence, or for maintaining the authority and impartiality of the judiciary.

dissemination of 'ideas' but of images containing personal, or even intimate, 'information' about that individual. Moreover, pictures published in the tabloid press were frequently snapped in an atmosphere of harassment that generated in the paparazzi's quarry a strong sense of intrusion, or even persecution.

The critical factor in balancing the protection of private life against freedom of expression, the Court held, was the contribution that the published photographs and articles made to a debate of general interest. The pictures of the princess were, it found, of a purely private nature, taken without her knowledge or consent, and, in some instances, in secret. They made no contribution to a debate of public interest given that she was not engaged in an official function, and that the photographs and articles related exclusively to details of her private life. Furthermore, while the public might have a right to information, including, in special circumstances, about the private life of public figures, they did not have such a right in this instance. It had no legitimate interest in knowing Princess Caroline's whereabouts or how she behaved in her private life—even in places that could not always be described as secluded. In the same way as there was a commercial interest for the magazines to publish the photographs and articles, those interests had, in the Court's view, to yield to the applicant's right to the effective protection of her private life.

A third appeal to the Court failed when a German magazine published an article relating to the recent trend among celebrities of renting out their holiday homes. This article went on to describe in detail the von Hannover family villa, which is located on an island off the Kenyan coast, setting out the furnishings, daily rental cost, and activities in the area. The article featured, alongside several photographs of the villa, a photograph showing Princess Caroline and her husband on holiday in an unidentifiable location.

The court unanimously held that the German Federal Court's refusal to grant an injunction prohibiting any further publication of this last photograph did not constitute a breach of the applicant's privacy rights as enshrined in Article 8. It applied five considerations by which to balance the right to respect for private life against the right to freedom of expression: whether the information contributes to a debate of general interest; the notoriety of the person concerned; the prior conduct of the person concerned; the content, form, and consequences of the publication; and the circumstances in which the photograph was taken.

Media misconduct

Following the disclosure of widespread hacking of mobile telephone voicemail, described in Chapter 1, the Leveson Inquiry Report in Britain was unequivocal in its condemnation of media misconduct:

> [T]he clearest message... is that, time and time again, there have been serious and uncorrected failures within parts of the national press that may have stretched from the criminal to the indefensibly unethical, from passing off fiction as fact to paying lip service to accuracy. In doing so, far from holding power to account... the press is exercising unaccountable power which nobody holds to account. In my view, the maintenance of the status quo is simply not an option; the need for change in internal but most importantly in external regulation has been powerfully identified.

The report was scathing in its appraisal of the performance, powers, and credibility of the existing self-regulatory body, the Press Complaints Commission (PCC), and recommended sweeping changes to its constitution. This attracted a degree of hostility in Britain, especially from the editors and proprietors of tabloid newspapers. It must be said, however, that self-regulation of the media (which exists in various forms in some fifty countries) tends to suffer from a number of deficiencies including, for example, that membership of the council is often voluntary and not all media organizations belong; the body cannot act pre-emptively to restrain publication or impose any financial sanctions; and it normally lacks the important principle of binding precedent. Despite these (and several other) shortcomings, a complaint to such a body has the benefits of economy, speed, and accessibility. Nor is a victim generally prevented from seeking a legal remedy after the body has issued its adjudication. In Britain, since the Human Rights Act 1998 became law, the PCC has achieved a significant measure of judicial recognition.

The English courts have recently been vigorously seeking to resolve the endless tussles between public figures and the media. Despite the absence of a privacy statute, the judges appear to have fashioned a remedy out of a cluster of analogous legal actions. However, this solution is unlikely to yield a coherent or durable solution to the problem.

Courting publicity?

Celebrities—stars of screen, radio, television, pop music, sport, and the catwalk—are regarded as fair game by the paparazzi. Members of the British royal family—most conspicuously, and tragically, the Princess of Wales—have long been preyed upon by the media.

It is persistently claimed that public figures forfeit their right to privacy. This contention is generally based on the following reasoning. It is asserted that celebrities relish publicity when it is favourable, but resent it when it is hostile. They cannot, it is argued, have it both ways. Second, the opinion is heard that the media have the right to 'put the record straight'. So, in the case of Naomi Campbell, since she had lied about her drug addiction, there was, the Court of Appeal held, a public interest in the press revealing the truth.

The first assertion—advanced, not surprisingly, by the media—is a specious application of the idiom: 'live by the sword, die by the sword'. It would sound the death knell for the protection of most public figures' private lives. The fact that celebrities court publicity—an inescapable feature of fame—cannot be allowed to annihilate their right to shield intimate features of their life from public view.

Nor is the second argument wholly persuasive. Suppose that a celebrity were HIV-positive or suffering from cancer. Can it really be the case that a legitimate desire on his or her part to deny that he or she is a sufferer of one of these diseases may be extinguished by the media's right to 'put the record straight'? If so, the protection of privacy becomes a fragile reed. Truth or falsity should not block the rights of those who dwell in the glare of public attention. There is a difference between 'publicity' and the disclosure of sensitive private information.

Freedom of expression

We are all publishers now. The Internet has created hitherto unthinkable opportunities for freedom of expression (and for eliciting information, see Figure 8). Bloggers proliferate at the rate of 120,000 a day. Social networking is the new form of community: Facebook has over a billion users; MySpace, around 36 million; and Twitter has almost 650 million active users who tweet an average of 58 million times a day. Yet, these astonishing developments notwithstanding, the central question remains the same. How is privacy to be reconciled with freedom of expression?

The electronic age has still to address Warren and Brandeis's entreaty (discussed in Chapter 3) that the law ought to prevent the distress caused by the gratuitous publication of private information (see Box 3).

What are the justifications for free speech in a democratic society? They tend to be based either on the positive consequences fostered by the exercise of the freedom or on the protection of individuals' right to express themselves. The former—consequentialist—argument usually draws on the case

joyoftech.com

8. Revealing personal information is often hard to resist.

Box 3 Gossip online

Even if gossip in cyberspace never bubbles up into the traditional press, it is more widely broadcast and more easily misinterpreted than it is in real space, resurrecting all of the stifling intimacy of a traditional society without the redeeming promise of being judged in context. The fact that gossip in cyberspace is recorded, permanently retrievable, and globally accessible increases the risk that an individual's public face will be threatened by past indiscretions. Gossip published on an Internet chat group may, in the short run, reach an audience that is no bigger than gossip over the back fence in a small

> town. But because Internet gossip, unlike individual memories, never fades, it can be resurrected in the future by those who don't know the individual in question, and thus are unable to put the information in a larger context. And unlike gossip in a small town, Internet gossip is hard to answer, because its potential audience is anonymous and unbounded.
>
> Jeffrey Rosen, *The Unwanted Gaze: The Destruction of Privacy in America*

made for free speech by John Milton (see Box 4), and John Stuart Mill. The latter—rights-based—argument (see later) conceives of speech as an integral part of an individual's right to self-fulfilment.

These principles tend invariably to be amalgamated, and even confused. So, for example, Thomas Emerson discerns the following four primary justifications that include both sorts of claim: individual self-fulfilment; attainment of the truth; securing the participation by members of society in social, including political, decision-making; and providing the means of maintaining the balance between stability and change in society.

Box 4 Truth versus falsehood

And though all the winds of doctrine were let loose to play on the earth, so Truth be in the field, we do injuriously by licensing and prohibiting misdoubt her strength. Let her and Falsehood grapple; who ever knew Truth put to the worse in a free and open encounter?

I cannot praise a fugitive and cloistered virtue, unexercised and unbreathed, that never sallies out and sees her adversary, but slinks out of the race, where that immortal garland is to be run for, not without dust and heat.

John Milton, *Areopagitica*

Champions of privacy, on the other hand, rely almost exclusively on rights-based arguments, as outlined in Chapter 2. But the extent to which the law may legitimately curtail speech that undermines an individual's privacy is often presented as a contest between these two heavyweights: freedom of speech versus privacy. But this may be mere shadow boxing. Why? Because 'at most points the law of privacy and the law sustaining a free press do not contradict each other. On the contrary, they are mutually supportive, in that both are vital features of the basic system of individual rights.'

The mist begins to clear once we focus our attention on the essential nature of privacy. When it is recognized that our core concern is the protection of personal information, the real character of the debate is illuminated. There are some positive signs therefore that the quest for the elusive equilibrium between privacy and free speech has produced some scepticism about the conventional approach that languishes in an incoherent concept of privacy.

Whose freedom?

Does freedom of speech protect the interests of the speaker or the listener? Or, to put it more portentously, is the justification individual- or community-based?

The former is rights-based, and argues for the interests in individual autonomy, dignity, self-fulfilment, and other values that the exercise of free speech safeguards or advances. The latter is community-based, and is consequentialist or utilitarian. It draws on democratic theory or the promotion of truth to support free speech as facilitating or encouraging the unfettered exchange of ideas, the dissemination of information, and other means of enlarging participation in self-government.

Freedom of speech and privacy are often regarded as rights or interests of the individual, and—sometimes in the same breath—as rights or interests of the community as a whole. And, even more troubling, free speech is regarded as one, and privacy the other, thereby rendering any 'balancing' of the two somewhat problematic! In respect of the interests of the individual, they generally share the same concerns. Indeed, the social functions of privacy are difficult to distinguish from those of freedom of expression, as mentioned above. To treat them both as individual rights would seem to be an important step towards simplifying the issue.

Policy and principle

Theories of freedom of expression that seek to protect the audience are generally arguments of policy, based on the importance of that freedom to the community. Those that advance the interests of the speaker, on the other hand, are generally arguments of principle which give primacy to the individual's self-fulfilment over the interests of the community. The jurist Ronald Dworkin has suggested that free speech is likely to receive stronger protection when it is regarded as safeguarding, as a matter of principle, the rights of the speaker. And privacy is, in its broad sense, also rights-based rather than goal-based. If this is correct, it would at least facilitate a greater symmetry in the balancing exercise.

Unfortunately, the matter is more complex than this. At first blush, this strategy would provide a logical basis for claiming that publications that harm other individuals cannot seriously be said to advance the speaker's or publisher's interest in self-fulfilment. Who is 'fulfilled' by the disclosure that a supermodel is a drug addict? And who is to say whether certain forms of speech are instrumental in achieving this object?

Moreover, the argument 'suffers from a failure to distinguish intellectual self-fulfilment from other wants and needs, and thus fails to support a distinct principle of free speech'. It is also founded on the principle of the free dissemination of *ideas* rather than *information*, which reduces its utility in the present context. And, most embarrassingly, the argument is hard to deploy in defence of *press* freedom, which appears to rest almost entirely on the interests of the community rather than those of the individual journalist, editor, or publisher.

What of the speaker's motives? It would not be unduly disingenuous to suggest that profit may be of some interest to newspaper editors and proprietors. And, as Eric Barendt remarks, 'a rigorous examination of motives to exclude speech made for profit would leave little immune from regulation'. Nor does the audience necessarily care; a good read is a good read whether its author is moved by greed or edification.

Truth

John Stuart Mill's celebrated argument from truth is based on the idea that any suppression of speech is an 'assumption of infallibility' and that only by the unrestricted circulation of ideas can the truth be revealed. But when taken to its logical conclusion, this would prevent any inroads being made into the exercise of the right to speak—at least truthfully. Apart from Mill's dubious supposition that there is an objective 'truth' out there, and his confidence in the dominance of reason, his theory makes the legal regulation of disclosures of personal information (as well as several other forms of speech that cause harm) extremely difficult to justify. It asserts that freedom of expression is a social good because it is the best process by which to advance knowledge and discover truth, starting from the premise that the soundest and most rational judgment is arrived at by considering all facts and arguments for and against. And, according to Emerson, this free marketplace of ideas should exist irrespective of how pernicious or false the new opinion appears to be 'because there is no way of suppressing the false without suppressing the true'.

But is the argument from truth really relevant to the protection of privacy? Frederick Schauer doubts whether truth is indeed ultimate and non-instrumental; does it not secure a 'deeper good' such as happiness or dignity? If truth is instrumental, then whether more truth causes a consequential strengthening of this deeper good is a question of fact and not an inexorable, logical certainty from definition. For Schauer, the argument from truth is an 'argument from knowledge'; an argument that the value in question is having people believe that things are in fact true.

Democracy

Free speech performs an essential function in promoting and maintaining democratic self-governance. This is an extension of the argument from truth, as the American political theorist Alexander Meiklejohn puts it:

> The principle of the freedom of speech springs from the necessities of the program of self-government. It is not a Law of Nature or Reason in the abstract. It is a deduction from the basic American agreement that public issues shall be decided by universal suffrage.

Yet, as in the case of the argument from truth, it must be queried how self-government is facilitated or advanced by the revelation of intimate private facts about, say, an individual's sexual proclivities? Is it 'speech' at all?

In some cases, such information may be relevant to self-government. Where, for instance, people acting through their democratically elected government consider a certain action to be sufficiently anti-social to constitute a criminal offence, then it is in the interest of self-governance that offenders are apprehended and punished. Similarly, where an individual holds a public office, and thereby actually acts on behalf of the people, representing and implementing their political opinions, any activity of that person which pertains directly to his or her fitness to perform that function is a legitimate interest of the community. Sadly, there are all too many examples of politicians championing 'family values' who are then exposed as adulterers or worse. A public interest test is capable of supporting freedom of expression in these cases. The argument from democracy should not be taken to justify unlimited freedom of speech in the privacy arena.

Media freedom

Arguments from democracy are in full flower here. For Milton and Blackstone it was the prior restraining of the press that represented the most sinister threat to freedom of speech. Sir William Blackstone, the 18th century jurist, declared:

> The liberty of the press is indeed essential to the nature of a free state; but this consists in laying no previous restraints upon publications and not in freedom from censure for criminal matter when published. Every free man has an undoubted right to lay what sentiments he pleases before the public: to forbid this, is to destroy the freedom of the press: but if he publishes what is improper, mischievous, or illegal, he must take the consequence of his own temerity.

Both the conception of the press and the boundaries of its freedom are, however, considerably wider today. Thus the term 'press' normally extends beyond newspapers and periodicals to include a far wider range of publications media: television, radio, and the Internet. Nor is the scope of press freedom restricted to prohibitions against 'prior constraint'.

The political justification for free speech is an application of the argument from truth. Mill's second hypothesis, it will be recalled, is the 'assumption of infallibility' that specifies the conditions under which we are able to have confidence in believing that what we think is true, actually is in fact true. The safest way to achieve this, the argument runs, is to accord individuals the freedom to debate ideas: to subject them to contradiction and refutation. Interference with this freedom diminishes our ability to arrive at rational beliefs.

This is a powerful idea, even if it may appear to be based on an idealized model of the political process in which there is active popular participation in government. A free press does have the potential to engender this awareness and to facilitate its exercise.

The appeal of the arguments from truth and from democracy is that they establish independent grounds for freedom of expression in a way that arguments based on the interests of the speaker do not. But the media publish much that, even by the most generous exercise of the imagination, is not remotely connected to these noble pursuits. Does this suggest that they are entitled to no special treatment? Arguments to support special treatment for the press tend to fall on stony judicial ground. A stronger case can plainly be made where, unlike the *Daily Mirror* in the Naomi Campbell case, the media offends decorum rather than the law. This argument may then be made to turn on the importance to the political process of the publication of a particular report. Accounts of the private lives of government ministers, officials, politicians, and even perhaps royalty, it could plausibly be claimed, warrant special treatment. Here, the nature of the message, and not the medium of its propagation, is the focal point of concern. This approach does not distinguish whether the freedom is exercised by the media, online, or in the pub. It has the additional merit of avoiding the problem of defining the 'press' or the 'media'.

The First Amendment

In the US, the issue of freedom of expression is debated against the background of the First Amendment's injunction that 'Congress shall make no law... abridging the freedom of speech, or of the press'. American courts and commentators have developed several theories of free speech, both rights-based and consequentialist, which seek to account for the exercise of freedom of expression in all its protean forms. Nevertheless, although it would be artificial to conceive of the problems encountered by the efforts to reconcile privacy and free speech as a discrete matter, the American law does appear to have developed the contours of a privacy/free speech theory.

In particular, there is a tendency to adopt a purposive construction of the First Amendment. This asks: what forms of speech or publication warrant protection by virtue of their contribution to the operation of political democracy. It has been employed in several decisions that distinguish, with variable consequences, between public figures and ordinary individuals. Indeed, the Supreme Court applied the principle adopted in the well-known libel case of *New York Times v Sullivan* to the privacy case of *Time, Inc. v Hill*. In the former decision, the Court expressed its philosophy in unequivocal terms:

> [W]e consider this case against the background of a profound national commitment to the principle that debate on public issues should be uninhibited, robust and wide open, and that it may well include vehement, caustic, and sometimes unpleasantly sharp attacks on government and public officials.

The chief purpose of the First Amendment is, in this approach, the protection of the right of all citizens to understand political issues in order that they might participate effectively in the operation of democratic government. This formula allows considerable scope for actions by private individuals who have been subjected to gratuitous publicity. In practice, however, it is frequently those who are in the public eye that—for this very reason—attract the attention of the tabloids. The difficult question which the theory is then required to answer is the extent to which such public figures are entitled to protection of aspects of their personal lives. And this, in turn, involves a delicate investigation of what features of a public figure's life may legitimately be exposed—in the furtherance of political debate. His sex life? Her health? Their finances?

Although this theory seeks to distinguish between voluntary and involuntary public figures, its application, except as a general rationale for the existence of the freedom of speech itself, provides uncertain guidance as to the respective rights and obligations in cases involving unwanted publicity. In the absence of an attempt to define the kinds of information in respect of which all individuals might *prima facie* expect to receive protection (even if such protection is subsequently to be outweighed by considerations of the public interest), one of the central purposes of recognizing an individual's interest in restricting information—the trust, candour, and confidence it fosters—is diminished.

Balancing competing interests

Is it possible to formulate a coherent theory of free speech which is both sufficiently broad to capture the complexities of the exercise of the freedom, and sufficiently specific to account for its variable applications? The argument from democracy attracts greater support than the Millian or autonomy-based theories, but all provide at best only the most general guidance in respect of the legitimate controls on the public disclosure of personal information by the media.

An interest-based theory that specifies the particular interests of the parties involved in the disclosure raises numerous difficulties (not unlike the interest-based accounts of privacy). And, while it is useful to distinguish, say, the 'personality' interests involved when private facts are published from the 'reputational' interests affected by defamatory publications, or the 'commercial' interests affected by breaches of confidence, this approach fails to explain which species of information warrant protection in the face of the competing claims of free speech.

The American Supreme Court has, in mediating between the two interests, resorted to the process of 'balancing' by which the interest in free speech is weighed against other interests such as national security, public order, and so on. If such interests are found to be 'compelling' or 'substantial', or where there is a 'clear and present danger' that the speech will cause significant harm to the public interest, the Court will uphold the restriction of free speech.

The dynamics of limitation

Emerson uses this phrase to describe the proposition that the public interest in the freedom of expression must fit into a 'more comprehensive scheme of social values and social goals'. So far, I have touched on the inapplicability of certain free speech justifications; I have allowed the right of privacy to escape unscathed. Where there is a genuine conflict between the two values, how is privacy to be protected? Or, in other words, why should free speech be subordinated to the protection of personal information?

In what circumstances might the absolute protection of free speech be moderated? Emerson suggests three. The first is where the injury is direct and peculiar to the individual, rather than one suffered in common with others. The second is when the interest is an intimate and personal one: embracing an area of privacy from which both the state and other individuals should be excluded. The third consideration is whether or not society leaves the burden of protecting the interest to the individual, by, for example recognizing that he or she has a legal cause of action.

In the first two circumstances, the harm is likely to be direct and irremediable. Moreover, if the individual has the burden of establishing his or her case, the resources of the state are less likely to be marshalled into a coherent apparatus for the restriction of free speech. He proposes that 'so long as the interest of privacy is genuine, the conditions of recovery clearly defined, and the remedy left to the individual suit, it is most unlikely that the balance will be tipped too far towards restriction of expression'.

Even against the background of the First Amendment, Emerson's approach is persuasive. And no less so in the context of the English law's constitutional silences as to safeguards for free speech. In the words of one senior judge:

> It cannot be too strongly emphasized that outside the established exceptions, or any new ones which Parliament may enact in accordance with its obligations under the Convention [for the Protection of Human Rights and Fundamental Freedoms], there is no question of balancing freedom of speech against other interests. It is a trump card which always wins.

The court nevertheless acknowledged, that 'a right of privacy may be a legitimate exception to freedom of speech'. And other judges have recognized that there are 'exceptional cases, where the intended publication is plainly unlawful and would inflict grave injury on innocent people or seriously impede the course of justice'. Another declared that 'Blackstone was concerned to prevent government interference with the press. The times of Blackstone are not relevant to the times of Mr Murdoch.'

The public interest

When is a matter in the public interest? Courts have struggled to formulate rational criteria by which to make this controversial judgment. Among the considerations that would seem to be relevant are the following: To whom was the information given? Is the victim a public figure? Was he or she in a public place? Is the information in the public domain? Did the victim consent to publication? How was the information acquired? Was it essential for the victim's identity to be revealed? Was the invasion a serious one? What were the publisher's motives in disclosing the information?

In the US, publishers need only to raise the defence of public interest or newsworthiness for it generally to demolish the protection against the gratuitous publication of private facts by the media. Thus in *Sidis v F.-R. Publishing Corporation*, discussed further on in this chapter, the court declared that 'at some point the public interest in obtaining information becomes dominant over the individual's desire for privacy'. The privilege is defined in the *Second Restatement of Torts* as extending to information 'of legitimate concern to the public'—a conclusion which is reached by weighing the competing interests of the public's right to know against the individual's right to keep private facts away from the public's gaze. This may be decided by the judge, as a matter of law, or, more often, by the jury, as a question of fact. The test embodied in the *Restatement*, reads as follows:

> In determining what comprises a matter of legitimate public interest, account must be taken of the customs and conventions of the community; and in the last analysis what is proper becomes a matter of the community mores. The line is to be drawn when the publicity ceases to be the giving of information to which the public is entitled, and becomes a morbid and sensational prying into private lives for its own sake, with which a reasonable member of the public, with decent standards, would say that he had no concern.

The categories of information which are newsworthy have steadily expanded as the courts have become increasingly conscious of the free speech implications of censoring accurate reporting. Sexual matters—understandably—dominate. This is illustrated by two Californian cases. In the first, an ex-marine became the subject of intense media interest when he foiled an assassination attempt on President Ford. The *San Francisco Chronicle* revealed that Sipple was a prominent member of the gay community, which indeed was true, but he brought an action under the tort of the public disclosure of private facts because he claimed that he had always kept his homosexuality private from his relatives. The court dismissed his action on two grounds. First, the information was already in the public domain; and, second, it held that the facts disclosed were newsworthy because the exposé was fuelled by the wish to combat the stereotyping of gays as 'timid, weak and unheroic', and to discuss the potential biases of the President (one newspaper had suggested that the President's reticence in thanking Sipple was on account of the latter's homosexuality).

In the other case, a newspaper article revealed that the first female student president of a Californian college, Diaz, was a transsexual. The court held that her transsexuality was a private fact and also that, although she was involved in a public controversy (in that she accused the college of misuse of student funds), the disclosure was irrelevant to that issue and, accordingly, not newsworthy. The court emphasized that the purpose of First Amendment protection was 'to keep the public informed so that they may make intelligent decisions on matters important to self-governing people'. It was further explained that 'the fact that she is a transsexual does not adversely reflect on her honesty or judgment. Nor does the fact that she was the first woman student body president, in itself, warrant that her entire private life be open to public inspection.'

How are these two decisions to be reconciled? The answer may lie in the tenor of the *Diaz* article. The newspaper argued that the report was intended to portray the 'changing roles of women in society', but it was clear from the tone of the article that the author's objective stopped at the 'stark revelation'. An important feature of both decisions is that the articles purported to portray alternative lifestyles. It is therefore arguable that, if the article about Diaz had seriously intended to portray the changing role of women in society, the court may have resisted calls for its censorship.

Celebrities

Our planet is star-struck. The most trivial item of gossip about a celebrity seems to excite huge interest and fascination. Newsstands are crammed with magazines devoted to the unremitting supply of these ephemeral, generally inane, facts. Does stardom extinguish privacy? Although the *American Restatement* comments that 'there may be some intimate details of her life, such as sexual relations, which even the actress is entitled to keep to herself', the decision in *Ann-Margret v High Society Magazine, Inc.* illustrates that this delicacy has not yet been fully embraced by the courts. In this court case, the actress was denied relief in respect of the publication of a nude photograph of herself, partly because the photograph was of 'a woman who has occupied the fantasies of many movie-goers' and therefore 'of great interest to many people'.

It is often claimed that courts simply accept the judgment of the press as to what is newsworthy. One writer contends that 'deference to the judgment of the press may actually be the appropriate and principled response to the newsworthiness enquiry'. But this neglects the reason why the subject is contentious at all. She observes that 'the economic survival of publishers and broadcasters depends upon their ability to provide a product that the public will buy', and argues that marketplace competition breeds into the papers a 'responsiveness to what substantial segments of the population want to know to cope with the society in which they live'.

The concept of public interest all too easily camouflages the commercial motives of the media (see Figure 9). Worse, it masquerades as the democratic exercise of consumer choice: we get the sensationalism we deserve. Both forms of cynical tabloidism neglect the consequences for individuals who happen to be public figures because they are unfortunate enough to be catapulted into the public eye.

A mores test

To evaluate what is 'highly offensive', the American courts have developed what has been called a 'mores test'. Thus, in *Melvin*

9. The actor, Hugh Grant, giving evidence at the Leveson Inquiry.

v Reid, the plaintiff's past as a prostitute and defendant in a sensational murder trial was revealed in a film called *The Red Kimono*, which was based on these events. She had, in the eight years since her acquittal, been accepted into 'respectable society', married, and was moving in a circle of friends who were ignorant of her past. Her action for the invasion of her privacy caused by the defendant's truthful disclosures was sustained by the California court (which had not hitherto recognized an action for invasion of privacy).

In *Sidis v F.-R. Publishing Corporation*, on the other hand, the plaintiff, a former child prodigy who, at 11, lectured in mathematics at Harvard, had become a recluse and devoted his time to studying the Okamakammessett Indians and collecting streetcar transfers. The *New Yorker* published an article, 'Where Are They Now? April Fool' written by James Thurber under a pseudonym. Details of Sidis's physical characteristics and mannerisms, the single room in which he lived, and his current activities were revealed. The magazine article acknowledged that Sidis had informed the reporter, who had tracked him down for the interview, that he lived in fear of publicity and changed jobs whenever his employer or fellow workers learned of his past. The New York District Court denied his action for invasion of privacy on the ground that it could find no decision 'which held the "right of privacy" to be violated by a newspaper or magazine publishing a correct account of one's life or doings...except under abnormal circumstances which did not exist in the case at bar'. On appeal, the Second Circuit affirmed the dismissal of the privacy action, but appeared to base its decision on a balancing of the offensiveness of the article with the public or private character of the plaintiff.

In neither *Melvin* nor *Sidis*, however, was there a proper attempt to consider the extent to which the information divulged was 'private'. The conceptually vague notions of 'community customs', 'newsworthiness', and the 'offensiveness' of the publication render these and many other decisions concerning 'public disclosure' unhelpful in an area of considerable constitutional importance. And this is equally true of the efforts by the Supreme Court to fix the boundaries of the First Amendment in respect of publications which affect the plaintiff's privacy. For example, in *Time, Inc. v Hill* the Court held that the plaintiff's action for invasion of privacy failed where he (and his family) had been the subject of a substantially false report. The defendant had published a description of a new play adapted from a novel which fictionalized the ordeal suffered by the plaintiff when he and his family were held hostage in their home by a group of escaped prisoners.

Adopting the test that it had applied in respect of defamation, the Supreme Court held, by a majority, that unless there was proof of actual malice (i.e. that the defendant had knowingly published an untrue report), the action would fail. Falsity alone did not deprive the defendant of his protection under the First Amendment—if the publication was newsworthy. And, since the 'opening of a new play linked to an actual incident is a matter of public interest', the plaintiff, because he was unable to show malice, failed. Yet it does seem that the decision was not really concerned with the public disclosure of private information—whether or not it was even a genuine libel action!

The future

There is no golden fleece. Enactment tomorrow, anywhere, of a comprehensive privacy statute would generate new problems for the judicial construction of victims' rights against unsolicited intrusions into private lives. Nor would these difficulties be diminished if the courts were to pursue a common law case-by-case route towards protection. The media would continue to be tested daily—albeit with more concentrated minds perhaps—as to whether stories were 'in the public interest'.

The quest for a just equilibrium will never end. The key issue is whether, as often seems to be the case, the interests of the individual are to be sacrificed at the altar of a contrived public interest? Opponents of legal, or even non-legal, checks on unwanted public disclosure are wont to depict the concern for a particular victim as being quaint or prudish. This is distinguished from the vigorous pursuit of the truth by the media. In many cases, of course, the media, like all commercial institutions, is moved by the interests of its shareholders, who may be less concerned about what is published than they are about the company balance sheet. While the media frequently concedes that it should resist publishing insensitive disclosures of private facts, it is hardly in a position to characterize such apprehensions as coming out of a sense of the pious or censorious.

There is nothing new about the law's struggle to keep abreast of technology. In this case, however, the contest may not be worth the candle. Attempts to control the Internet—its operation or content—have been notoriously unsuccessful. Its anarchy and resistance to regulation is, in the minds of many, the principal source of its power and attraction. Inevitably, the advances in electronic media will continue to test the appropriateness of existing standards. Can the same regulation that is applied, for example, to broadcasting be applied to computer networks?

The print media appears to enjoy a preferred position, and seems less susceptible to regulation than the electronic word, although the latter is now already the dominant means of communication in advanced societies. As the differences between the various forms of media dissolve, there is clearly a need to establish a regime that recognizes the rights of both the users and the operators of the new technology. It can no longer matter whether the information you receive appears in the pages of your newspaper or online.

Nevertheless, although the form in which a message is transmitted may cease to be a significant factor, users of the Internet experience communication in a fundamentally different way from other electronic media. Thus, in the case of television and radio, the number of speakers is limited by the available spectrum, the ability to speak is restricted by the high cost of speaking, and listeners are (at least in general) merely passive recipients of these communications. With the Internet, on the other hand, the number of speakers is infinite and interactivity is standard. Unlike with television and radio, an online speaker can reach the entire world and yet still be able to direct his or her speech to particular individuals who share an interest in a particular subject.

Some contend that our digital world requires a modified, or even a new, approach in the pursuit of the elusive equilibrium between privacy and free speech. But, although the Internet is susceptible to considerably less control than the printed media, the central question is inescapable: how is the right to privacy to be reconciled with freedom of expression? Our electronic age has still to address Warren and Brandeis's entreaty (discussed in Chapter 3) that the law ought to prevent or redress the anguish caused by the gratuitous publication of private information.

In fact, the Internet constitutes Emerson's quintessential 'free marketplace of ideas': it provides an authentic rough-and-tumble environment of critical scepticism with the freedom to express the uncomfortable, the unpalatable, and the unconventional. The marketplace should exist, Emerson argued, irrespective of how pernicious or false the new opinion appears to be because there is no way of suppressing the false without suppressing the true. Such a model may nevertheless preserve the rights of those harmed by the exercise of this liberty, including their right to privacy. The protection of anonymous speech is likely to attract greater attention as a vital element both of free speech and privacy in cyberspace. If treated as analogous to public space, it may be that if you object to what you see or hear online, you may simply have to look away, as pedestrians do when offended by a billboard.

Privacy advocates may well include enemies of free speech, but that is no more a legitimate argument against them than the contention that advocates of free speech include avaricious newspaper proprietors. The power of the media lobby can, however, never be underestimated. How many politicians, whose careers often hang by a slender thread, wish to invite the animosity of the media by championing curbs on reporting of what has come to be called 'bonk journalism'? The media, while quick to condemn the exposure of private lives in the name of the public interest, inevitably closes ranks against legislation. Unhappily, although most tabloids preach family values, they often demonstrate little concern or respect for the families of their victims.

Chapter 5
Data protection

Information is no longer merely power. It is big business. In recent years the fastest growing component of international trade has been the service sector. It accounts for more than a third of world trade—and it continues to expand. It is a commonplace to identify as a central feature of modern industrialized societies their dependence on the storage of information. The use of computers facilitates, of course, considerably greater efficiency and velocity in the collection, storage, use, retrieval, and transfer of information.

The routine functions of government and private institutions require a constant stream of data about us in order to administer effectively the countless services that are an essential ingredient of contemporary life. The provision of health services, social security, credit, insurance, and the prevention and detection of crime assume the availability of a substantial quantity of personal data and, hence, a readiness by individuals to supply it. The computerization of this—often highly sensitive—information intensifies the risks of its misuse. Or indeed its careless loss—which seems to occur with alarming frequency.

Genesis

The dawn of information technology in the 1960s witnessed growing anxiety about the perceived threats posed by the

uncontrolled collection, storage, and use of personal data.
The fear of Big Brother provoked calls in several countries
for the regulation of these potentially intrusive activities. The
first data-protection law was enacted in the German state of
Hesse in 1970. This was followed by national legislation in
Sweden (1973), the US (1974), Germany (1977), and France
(1978).

Out of this early chrysalis were born two key international
instruments: the Council of Europe's 1981 Convention for the
Protection of Individuals with regard to the Automatic Processing
of Personal Data, and the 1980 Organisation for Economic
Co-operation and Development (OECD) Guidelines Governing
the Protection of Privacy and Transborder Data Flows of Personal
Data. These documents formulated explicit rules governing the
complete process of managing electronic data. At the core of
data-protection legislation, since the OECD guidelines, is the
proposition that data relating to an identifiable individual should
not be collected in the absence of a genuine purpose and the
consent of the individual concerned (see Box 5).

At a slightly higher level of abstraction, it encapsulates the principle
of what the German Constitutional Court has called 'informational
self-determination'—an ideal that expresses a fundamental
democratic ideal.

Adherence to or, more precisely, enforcement of this objective
(and the associated rights of access and correction) has been mixed
in the 40 or so jurisdictions that have enacted data-protection
legislation. Most of these statutes draw on the two international
instruments mentioned above. Article 1 of the Council of Europe's
Convention on the Protection of Individuals with Regard to
Automatic Processing of Personal Data states that its purpose is:

> to secure in the territory of each Party for every individual, whatever
> his nationality or residence, respect for his rights and fundamental

Box 5 The OECD principles

Collection Limitation Principle

There should be limits to the collection of personal data and any such data should be obtained by lawful and fair means and, where appropriate, with the knowledge or consent of the data subject.

Data Quality Principle

Personal data should be relevant to the purposes for which they are to be used, and, to the extent necessary for those purposes, should be accurate, complete and kept up-to-date.

Purpose Specification Principle

The purposes for which personal data are collected should be specified not later than at the time of data collection and the subsequent use limited to the fulfilment of those purposes or such others as are not incompatible with those purposes and as are specified on each occasion of change of purpose.

Use Limitation Principle

Personal data should not be disclosed, made available or otherwise used for purposes other than those specified in accordance with Paragraph 9 except:

a) with the consent of the data subject; or

b) by the authority of law.

Security Safeguards Principle

Personal data should be protected by reasonable security safeguards against such risks as loss or unauthorized access, destruction, use, modification or disclosure of data.

Openness Principle

There should be a general policy of openness about developments, practices and policies with respect to personal data. Means should be readily available of establishing the existence and nature of personal data, and the main purposes of their use, as well as the identity and usual residence of the data controller.

Individual Participation Principle

An individual should have the right:

a) to obtain from a data controller, or otherwise, confirmation of whether or not the data controller has data relating to him;

b) to have communicated to him, data relating to him
   (i) within a reasonable time;
   (ii) at a charge, if any, that is not excessive;
   (iii) in a reasonable manner; and
   (iv) in a form that is readily intelligible to him;

c) to be given reasons if a request made under subparagraphs (a) and (b) is denied, and to be able to challenge such denial; and

d) to challenge data relating to him and, if the challenge is successful to have the data erased, rectified, completed or amended.

Accountability Principle

A data controller should be accountable for complying with measures which give effect to the principles stated above.

OECD Guidelines on the Protection of Privacy and Transborder Flows of Personal Data, Part Two (adopted 23 September 1980)

freedoms, and in particular his right to privacy, with regard to automatic processing of personal data relating to him ('data protection').

The importance of these principles cannot be overstated. In particular, of the use limitation and purpose specification principles are crucial canons of fair information practice. Together with the principle that personal data shall be collected by means that are fair and lawful, they provide a framework for safeguarding the use and disclosure of such data, but also (in the fair collection principle) for limiting intrusive activities such as the interception of email messages. Personal data may be used or disclosed only for the purposes for which the data were collected or for some directly related purposes, unless the data subject consents. This key precept goes a long way towards regulating the misuse of personal data on the Internet. But it requires rejuvenation where it already exists and urgent adoption where it does so only partially (most conspicuously in the US).

The enactment of data-protection legislation is driven only partly by altruism. The new information technology disintegrates national borders; international traffic in personal data is a routine feature of commercial life. The protection afforded to personal data in Country A is, in a digital world, rendered nugatory when it is retrieved on a computer in Country B in which there are no controls over its use. Hence, states with data-protection laws frequently proscribe the transfer of data to countries that lack them. Indeed, the EU has in one of its several directives explicitly sought to annihilate these 'data havens'. Without data-protection legislation, countries risk being shut out of the rapidly expanding information business.

Implementation of the Directive is in the hands of the Working Party on the Protection of Individuals (generally known as the Article 29 Working Party) which comprises representatives of the various data-protection agencies in each member state.

In 2012 it proposed comprehensive reform of its 1995 data-protection rules (see Box 6) to strengthen online privacy rights. The Commission's proposals will be passed to the European Parliament and EU Member States (meeting in the Council of Ministers) for deliberation. They will take effect two years after their eventual adoption. An important deficiency of the 1995 rules is their differential interpretation and application. The new order

Box 6 EU Directive on the processing of personal data

Article 3

1. This Directive shall apply to the processing of personal data wholly or partly by automatic means, and to the processing otherwise than by automatic means of personal data which form part of a filing system or are intended to form part of a filing system.

2. This Directive shall not apply to the processing of personal data: in the course of an activity which falls outside the scope of Community law,...and in any case to processing operations concerning public security, defence, State security (including the economic well-being of the State when the processing operation relates to State security matters) and the activities of the State in areas of criminal law, by a natural person in the course of a purely personal or household activity.

Article 6

1. Membering States shall provide that personal data must be:
   (a) processed fairly and lawfully;
   (b) collected for specified, explicit and legitimate purposes and not further processed in a way incompatible with those purposes. Further processing of data for historical, statistical or scientific purposes shall not be considered as incompatible provided that Member States provide appropriate safeguards;
   (c) adequate, relevant and not excessive in relation to the purposes for which they are collected and/or further processed;
   (d) accurate and, where necessary, kept up to date; every reasonable step must be taken to ensure that data

(*continued*)

which are inaccurate or incomplete, having regard to
the purposes for which they were collected or for which
they are further processed, are erased or rectified;
(e) kept in a form which permits identification of data
subjects for no longer than is necessary for the purposes
for which the data were collected or for which they are
further processed. Member States shall lay down
appropriate safeguards for personal data stored for
longer periods for historical, statistical or scientific use.

Directive of the European Parliament and Council of 24 October 1995

seeks to eliminate the current fragmentation (and its expensive
administrative burdens), and to help reinforce consumer confidence
in online services.

The EU Commission's proposals update and modernize the
principles enshrined in the 1995 Data Protection Directive to
guarantee privacy rights in the future. They include a policy
communication setting out the Commission's objectives and two
legislative proposals: a Regulation formulating a general EU
framework for data protection, and a Directive on protecting
personal data processed for the purposes of prevention, detection,
investigation, or prosecution of criminal offences.

Instead of the current costly obligation of companies to notify all
data-protection activities to data-protection supervisors the
Regulation provides for increased responsibility and accountability
for those processing personal data. For example, companies and
organizations will be required to inform the national supervisory
authority of serious data breaches as soon as possible (if feasible,
within twenty-four hours). It provides also that organizations will

now deal with a single national data-protection authority in the EU country where they are based. Wherever consent is required for data to be processed, it must be given explicitly rather than assumed.

Amongst other reforms, the Regulation stipulates that data subjects will have easier access to their own data and be able to transfer personal data from one service provider to another more easily (the right to 'data portability'). Recently the European Court of Justice recognized the 'right to be forgotten' to enable users to delete their data if there are no legitimate grounds for retaining them. In a controversial, and potentially far-reaching, decision, it decided that the Directive supported the applicant's claim against Google to have an old newspaper report on his financial history deleted. The court held that Google, despite being a search engine, was a 'controller' of the data it processes and provides. Data subjects were therefore able to request that search engines delete personal data from their search results, and, should they decline, to pursue legal action or complain to their data-protection authority.

The effect of the judgment is to render search engine operators responsible, as distinct from the original web page publishers, for removing information on data subjects from search engine results even where the publication on the original pages might be lawful. And the court added that the right to demand rectification, erasure, or blocking of data was not confined to where the data were inaccurate, but extended to circumstances in which the processing was unlawful for any other reason, including non-compliance with any other ground in the Directive relating to data quality or criteria for data processing, or in the context of the right to object to data processing on 'compelling legitimate grounds'. It acknowledged that this right had to be balanced against other rights, especially freedom of expression, but the public interest in the information was relevant only where the data subject was a public figure.

The judges recognized that the Directive's requirements that personal data must be retained for limited periods—only for as long as they are relevant—amounts to a form of the 'right to be forgotten'. A number of intriguing questions remain open. For example, when do personal data become irrelevant? Who is a public figure?

Within a few days of the ruling, hundreds of deletion requests were received by Google, including from an ex-politician seeking re-election, a convicted paedophile, and a medical doctor. In the following months, tens of thousands of requests followed. Almost a third related to fraud one-fifth concerned serious crime, and 12 per cent were connected to child pornography arrests. Serious concern has been expressed that the ruling will result in censorship and will limit freedom of expression.

An important element in the new regime is the application of EU rules where personal data are handled abroad by companies that are active in the EU market and that offer their services to EU citizens. Independent national data-protection authorities will be strengthened in order better to enforce the EU rules at home. They will be empowered to fine companies up to one million Euros (or up to 2 per cent of its global annual turnover).

The essentials of data protection

At the heart of any data-protection law lies the principle that personal data shall be collected by means that are 'lawful and fair in the circumstances of the case', to use the language of Hong Kong's Personal Data (Privacy) Ordinance of 1995, which will serve as an example here. In respect of the use and disclosure of such data, they may be used or disclosed only for the purposes for which the data were collected or for some directly related purposes, unless the data subject consents otherwise.

These provisions are buttressed by six 'data-protection principles' which are, in effect, the main cog of the legislative machinery.

While they seek to protect personal data, new threats are periodically generated that require continual review of the effectiveness of these principles. Briefly, the first principle prohibits the collection of data unless they are collected for a lawful purpose directly related to a function or activity of the data user who is to use the data, and that are adequate but not excessive in relation to that purpose. Personal data may be collected only by lawful and fair means. This requires a data user to inform the data subject of the purpose for which the data are to be used, the classes of persons to whom the data may be transferred, whether it is obligatory or voluntary for the data subject to supply the data, the consequences of failure to supply the data; and that the data subject has the right to request access to and correction of the data. The widespread use of cookies and tracking may undermine this principle of 'fair and lawful' collection. The EU's 'cookie directive' is discussed later.

The second principle requires data users to ensure that the data held are accurate and up to date. If in doubt, the data user should discontinue using the data at once. The user should not retain the data any longer than is necessary for the purpose for which they were collected. The excessive retention of personal data has attracted the attention of the European Court of Justice (discussed later in this chapter). The third principle provides that without the prescribed consent of the data subject, personal data may not be used for any purpose other than the purpose for which the data were to be used at the time of their collection.

Fourth, data users are obliged to take appropriate security measures to protect personal data. They must ensure that they are adequately protected against unauthorized or accidental access, processing, erasure, or use by others lacking authority. The fifth principle relates to the publicity a data user is required to give to the kind of personal data it holds, and its policies and practices in respect of the handling of personal data. This is normally achieved by a 'privacy policy statement' that includes details of the accuracy, retention period, security, and use of the data, as well as measures taken regarding data access and data correction requests. The advent of 'cloud computing' poses new challenges to the security of personal data. This fairly recent development creates a network that facilitates the simultaneous running of programs or applications on numerous computers. It is not without its practical and security drawbacks. Among the former is its dependence on the Internet—its connection, efficiency, and speed. In respect of the latter, the Snowden revelations invite concerns about the safety of the data, especially since cloud data are accessible online from anywhere in the world; they are therefore vulnerable to attack by hackers, disgruntled employees, or through careless login security. The final principle relates to the data subject's right to obtain access to personal data about him or her and to request a copy of such personal data held by that data user. Should the data turn out to be inaccurate, the data subject has the right to request the data user to correct the record.

A victim of intrusion or disclosure may complain to the Privacy Commissioner for Personal Data of a contravention of these principles. He or she has the power to issue an 'enforcement notice' to compel compliance with the law. Failure to comply with such a notice is an offence punishable on conviction by a fine and two years' imprisonment. The legislation provides also for compensation, including damages for injury to feelings.

A crucial element of the law is the power vested in the privacy commissioner to approve codes of practice to provide 'practical guidance' to both data users and data subjects. Those issued so far by the commissioner are substantial documents that are a product of detailed and lengthy consultation with the appropriate parties. Moreover, while the statute provides that a failure by a data user to observe any part of a code shall not render it liable to civil or criminal proceedings, an allegation in such proceedings that a data user has failed to follow the code is admissible as evidence.

What are 'personal data'?

The starting point of any data-protection law is the concept of 'personal data' or, in some statutes, 'personal information'. The term has been used numerous times in this book, but what precisely does it include? Though there are differences between domestic statutes, they share a fairly broadly defined notion of the phrase. Article 2(a) of the EU Directive employs the following formulation:

> [A]ny information relating to an identified or identifiable individual natural person ('data subject'); an identifiable individual is one who can be identified directly or indirectly, in particular by reference to an identification number or to one or more factors specific to his physical, physiological, mental, economic, cultural or social identity.

But what of data generated by cookies or RFID tags embedded in products or clothing? They do not necessarily refer to an individual, but since they facilitate decisions about a person, they warrant protection under the rubric of personal data.

Cookies directive

This was introduced in 2009 ostensibly to require informed consent to be obtained for any cookie installed on a computer unless 'strictly necessary for the delivery of a service requested by the user'. In 2012 European data-protection authorities (as part of the Article 29 Working Party) adopted an opinion that suggests that some cookie uses might be exempt from the requirement to gain consent. This includes cookies used to keep track of a user's input when filling online forms or as a shopping cart, multimedia player session cookies, and user interface customization cookies such as language preference. Users now notice a banner above websites requesting users to click to accept cookies. Needless to say, this is an almost worthless method by which to control the use of cookies.

'Personal data' and the European Directive

Although the definition of personal data in existing legislation manifestly incorporates information the obtaining or disclosure of which would constitute what might properly be called an invasion of privacy, its wide sweep neglects these issues. My own view is that it is principally information that is intimate or confidential that warrants protection in the name of privacy. But while the Directive, and domestic data-protection legislation, neglects this species of information, it does not altogether ignore it, as we shall see.

Despite the fact that any data-protection regime extends well beyond the information of an essentially private kind, and their (perhaps inevitable) procedural, rather than substantive, nature, they provide useful signposts to the more effective resolution of the challenges, especially of electronic privacy.

Article 25 of the European Directive specifies that any transfer of personal data that are being processed or are to be processed after their transfer must attract an adequate level of protection by the jurisdiction to which they are sent. The adequacy of protection is to be evaluated by reference to the nature of the data, the purpose and duration of the proposed processing, the country of origin and of final destination, the general or sectoral regulation in the jurisdiction in question, and the nature and scope of security measures. This immediately endangered the future of business in the largest market on earth, the US. I return to this difficulty below, under the subheading The American enigma.

Sensitive data

Certain items of personal information are intrinsically more sensitive than others, and therefore warrant stronger protection. What might these types of information be? Article 8 of the European Directive requires Member States to prohibit the processing of personal data 'revealing racial or ethnic origin, political opinions, religious or philosophical beliefs, trade union membership, and the processing of data concerning health or sex life'. This restriction is, however, subject to a number of exceptions including, unless domestic legislation explicitly provides otherwise, the provision by the data subject of explicit consent to such processing. It is also permissible when necessary to protect the rights and duties of the controller in the field of employment law, or to protect the 'vital interests' of the data subject.

This is echoed in the legislation of other European jurisdictions. The UK's Data Protection Act of 1998 classifies as 'sensitive' information relating to the data subject's racial or ethnic origin, political opinions, religious or similar beliefs, membership of a trade union, physical or mental health, sexual life, the commission or alleged commission of any offence, or any proceedings for any offence committed or alleged to have been committed.

Any inventory such as these clearly requires interpretation. Data about the twisted ankle that sent you to the hospital is plainly less sensitive than your HIV-positive status. But a modest degree of common sense ought to ensure that distinctions such as this are drawn.

In view of their high sensitivity, preserving the privacy of medical records is particularly critical. A growing problem concerns the significant number of non-medical personnel who have access to patients' data. They are not always subject to a strict duty of confidence.

Recently, the European Court of Human Rights penalized the government of Finland for its failure to protect medical patient data held by a hospital against the risk of unauthorized access. The judgment establishes a connection between the right to privacy under human rights law and the protection of personal information. It held that Article 8 includes a positive duty to ensure the security of personal data. The hospital's filing system contravened Finland's own law that requires hospitals to secure personal data against unauthorized access. The petitioner, a nurse at the hospital where she was being treated for HIV, suspected that her co-workers had discovered that she was HIV-positive by reading her confidential medical records. Although the hospital rules prohibited access to these files, save for purposes of treatment, in practice the records of patients were accessible to all hospital staff.

The Court held that the mere fact that the hospital had an insecure medical records system was sufficient to render it liable for the otherwise unexplained disclosure of the nurse's private medical data.

Equally troubling is the reckless loss of sensitive data stored on disks or memory sticks. In one recent instance, for example, disks containing personal information on almost 18,000 National Health Service patients went missing from a North London hospital. The hospital admitted that the disks were lost when they were put in the post!

The records of AIDS patients or those who are HIV-positive are especially sensitive. A number of arguments have, however, been raised to justify the violation of these patients' medical confidentiality. It is urged, in particular, that in order to contain the spread of the disease it may be necessary for doctors to report cases to public health authorities. Indeed, in some jurisdictions, AIDS is a notifiable disease and therefore a legal duty arises to inform authorities of its appearance. The requirement of accurate information is plainly important if research into the causes and proliferation of AIDS (or the Ebola virus) is to be effectively conducted. But there is no compelling reason why such data cannot almost always be anonymous. Given the traumatic consequences that their disclosure can produce, the onus should be on the health authority to demonstrate that the benefits outweigh patients' rights to confidentiality.

Indeed, the failure to protect adequately these data may well be counter-productive; many will simply be deterred from being tested for the virus. This will dry up sources of information and, at the same time, contribute indirectly to the further spread of the illness.

Other elementary failures in the security of medical data inspire little confidence in the proper enforcement of the Data Protection Act. A recent survey by two doctors at a top London hospital revealed that three-quarters of them carried unsecured memory sticks with confidential data. Hospital doctors routinely carry memory sticks containing names, diagnoses, X-rays, and treatment details. Of the 105 doctors at their hospital, 92 held memory sticks, with 79 of them containing confidential information. Only five of those were protected by passwords.

Digital data

The ubiquity of computers and computer networks facilitates almost instant storage, retrieval, and transfer of data—a far cry from the world of manual filing systems. More spectacularly, efforts to control the Internet, its operation, or content, have been conspicuously unsuccessful. Indeed, its anarchy and resistance to regulation are widely vaunted as its very strength and appeal. Apart from the problem of when it is reasonable to expect that one's conversations are private, the nature of communication on the Internet generates different issues and expectations, and, hence, the need for different solutions.

While the monitoring of digital telephone systems (described in Chapter 1) may appear to be similar to the sending and receiving of email, the use of the Internet poses intractable challenges to regulation. For example, while it is simple to monitor my telephone calls or intercept my letters, the culture of the Internet encourages a range of activities whose observation presents irresistible opportunities for those who wish to supervise or control the private and the sensitive.

Data protection and privacy

But, you are entitled to ask, what does data protection have to do with privacy? The relationship between the two is not immediately obvious. They plainly overlap; indeed, the latter is routinely invoked as the interest that animates the former. But—even in our information society—it is not always individual privacy that is violated by the collection, use, storage, or transfer of personal data. This is not merely because 'personal data' is widely defined in data-protection statutes to include information about a 'person' that is not necessarily 'private'. The simple answer is that in seeking to protect this class of data, information of a genuinely private nature is willy-nilly caught in the net.

Indeed, it is not wholly implausible to suggest that a number of the problems of defining privacy that we have encountered might be more practically resolved under the data-protection umbrella.

Think of the cases of Princess Caroline that were discussed in Chapter 4. The European Court of Human Rights considered them under the rubric of Article 8's so-called privacy clause in the European Convention. The central issue was the lawfulness of surreptitious photography in a public place. Data-protection statutes are not fashioned to provide comprehensive protection for individual privacy, but they routinely stipulate that personal data must be collected by means that are both lawful and fair. Such legislation thus affords incidental protection to privacy.

The American enigma

Despite—or perhaps because of—the magnitude of its information market, the US has resisted the adoption of data-protection legislation along European lines—at least in the private sector. Its approach of self-regulation is in stark contrast to the comprehensive approach of the EU model. This is, in part, attributable to a political culture that eschews vigorous regulatory bodies—a situation all too evident in the context of the credit crisis of 2008. It is hard to visualize the approval of the appointment of an independent Federal privacy commissioner.

To avoid a trade war with Europe, the US created the tranquil-sounding 'Safe Harbor' framework (see Box 7). The scheme was designed to satisfy the EU that US companies endorsing the scheme would offer adequate privacy protection as defined by the EU data-protection directive. This compromise was approved by the EU in 2000.

The scheme has attracted a disappointingly small number of American companies as they dislike the perceived burden it imposes upon them. The EU Commission has observed that a number of US companies fail to abide by the requirement, stating in their publicly available privacy policy that they comply with the seven principles. In addition, these privacy statements do not generally include all the principles or they translate them incorrectly. A significant deficiency in the implementation of the 'Safe Harbor'

Box 7 Unsafe harbour?

Perhaps because of its very lack of teeth, Safe Harbor is today regarded as tantamount to a dead letter. Most organizations importing personal data into the United States . . . appear simply to disregard the measure. One consultant who advises corporate clients on privacy issues told me that he recommends that they do exactly this—on the assumption that enforcement is so lax that noncompliance is unlikely to bring any sanctions.

J.B. Rule, *Privacy in Peril*

policy is the absence of a complaint enforcement mechanism by those companies that have adopted the system.

Protecting personal data online

The digital world we have created will soon comprise a fibre-optic network that carries—in digital bits—an almost infinite number of television channels, home shopping and banking, interactive entertainment and video games, computer databases, and commercial transactions. This broadband communications network will link households, businesses, and schools to a plethora of information resources. When personal information assumes the form of bits, its vulnerability to misuse, particularly on the Internet, is self-evident.

We have produced a multifunctional telecommunication network that links all existing networks that previously were independent. Moreover, what used to be unifunctional, immobile, and large hardware is now multifunctional, portable, and diminutive: my iPhone allows me to send and receive email, buy and sell, watch television, read newspapers, and so on.

The power of computers grows at an astonishing velocity; according to so-called 'Moore's Law', the capacity of a computer is doubled every eighteen months, while its price is unaffected. In other words, after a period of fifteen years, the processing and storage capabilities of our computers are increased by a factor of 1,000.

In 2012 the Obama Administration announced the introduction of a 'Consumer Privacy Bill of Rights' (see Box 8). It seeks to provide Internet users with greater control over how their personal information is used online, and to assist businesses to maintain consumer trust. In addition, advertising networks stated that leading Internet companies and online advertising networks were committing to act on 'Do Not Track' technology in most major web browsers to limit online tracking. Companies that provide almost

Box 8 The US 'Consumer Privacy Bill of Rights'

Individual Control: Consumers have a right to exercise control over what personal data organizations collect from them and how they use it.

Transparency: Consumers have a right to easily understandable information about privacy and security practices.

Respect for Context: Consumers have a right to expect that organizations will collect, use, and disclose personal data in ways that are consistent with the context in which consumers provide the data.

Security: Consumers have a right to secure and responsible handling of personal data.

Access and Accuracy: Consumers have a right to access and correct personal data in usable formats, in a manner that is appropriate to the sensitivity of the data and the risk of adverse consequences to consumers if the data are inaccurate.

Focused Collection: Consumers have a right to reasonable limits on the personal data that companies collect and retain.

Accountability: Consumers have a right to have personal data handled by companies with appropriate measures in place to assure they adhere to the Consumer Privacy Bill of Rights.

90 per cent of online behavioural advertisements, including Google, Yahoo!, Microsoft, and AOL, agreed to comply when consumers elect to control online tracking.

The advertising industry also undertook not to release consumers' browsing data to companies who might use it for purposes other than advertising, such as employers or insurers. Two years later, the Bill of Rights had not come into force to the dismay of a coalition of more than three dozen privacy groups that urged the

White House to go further and introduce a federal law codifying the various methods by which privacy is protected in the US.

Anonymity and identity

Anonymity is, as was discussed in Chapter 1, an important value. But it is not necessarily absolute anonymity that I seek. Instead, it is what Yves Poullet, director of the CRID (*Centre de Recherches Informatique et Droit*), calls 'functional non-identifiability' in respect of my message to any particular individual. The notion of anonymity should perhaps therefore be replaced by 'pseudonymity' or 'non-identifiability'. This right cannot, of course, be absolute. A balance must be struck with the demands of national security, defence, and the detection and prosecution of crime. This is possible by the use of 'pseudo-identities' furnished to individuals by specialist service providers who may only reveal a user's actual identity when required to do so by the law.

Conventional accounts—understandably—neglect the value and importance of anonymity as a feature of the 'new privacy'. The instability of the subject is a central theme of post-modernism. The Internet appears as a living testament to the ideas of the absence of a universal, unitary truth, and the contingency and diversity of the self that emerge in the writings of post-modern icons such as Jacques Lacan.

The fluidity of identity on the Internet is among its chief attractions, but there may be increasing pressure to establish who the sender is, especially for commercial purposes. Digital authentication is likely to grow in importance as more business is conducted online.

The future of data protection

The current data-protection regime sketched above is no panacea. It is ill-equipped to cope with the countless challenges to privacy by the Internet and technological advances in RFID, GPSs, mobile

Box 9 Global privacy standards

European and other countries with data privacy laws should continue to put pressure on US and Chinese business and government agencies to ensure that they comply with what is an increasingly global standard for data privacy. Applying pressure is particularly important when the operation of US and Chinese businesses involves the personal data of citizens of other countries. Respect for their domestic prerogatives should not be confused with any need to reduce fundamental aspects of global data privacy standards.

N. Witzleb, D. Lindsay, M. Paterson, S. Rodrick, *Emerging Challenges in Privacy Law: Comparative Perspectives*

telephony, and so on (see Box 9). These developments are admirably described by Poullet, who postulates a new suite of principles to manage these frequently unsettling developments.

The ubiquity and multi-functionality of electronic communication service environments, as well as their interactivity, the international character of networks, services, and equipment producers, and the absence of transparency in terminal and network functioning all jeopardize online privacy (for degrees of international protection, see Figure 10). Poullet accordingly proposes a number of 21st century principles that include the principle of encryption and reversible anonymity. This is of critical importance in providing protection against access to the content of our communications. Encryption software has become affordable to the ordinary computer user.

Another principle is that of encouraging technological approaches compatible with or improving the situation of legally protected persons. This could involve requiring that both software and hardware provide the necessary tools to comply with data-protection

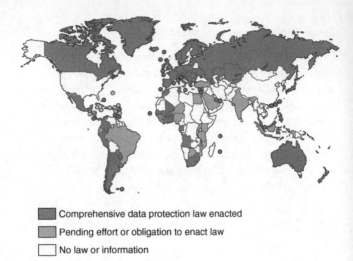

■ Comprehensive data protection law enacted

■ Pending effort or obligation to enact law

□ No law or information

10. Personal information is accorded varying degrees of protection across the globe.

rules. They ought to include maximum protective features as standard.

This obligation also applies to those who process personal data to select the most appropriate technology for minimizing the threat to privacy. The development of the PETs described in Chapter 1, ought to be encouraged and subsidized, voluntary certification and accreditation systems established, and PETs made available at reasonable prices.

Hardware should operate transparently; users should have complete control over data sent and received. They ought, for example, to be able to ascertain easily the extent of chattering on their computers, what files have been received, their purpose, and their senders and recipients. Anyone who has attempted to block pop-up windows will know how frustratingly difficult this process can be. Omitting to activate a cookie suppressor cannot be construed as carte blanche consent to their installation.

Our online lives warrant protection equivalent to the consumer laws that we enjoy in the material world. Why should surfers be expected to tolerate profiling, spamming, differential access to services, and so on? Online consumer protection legislation could open the door to a range of services, including the specification of the duties of Internet service providers, search engines, databases, as well as measures to prevent unfair competition and commercial practices. Moreover, as Poullet argues, why should product liability for hardware and software not extend beyond physical and financial harm to incorporate infringements of data-protection norms?

The advent of Web 2.0 has generated a massive explosion in social networking sites such as Facebook and MySpace, video-sharing sites like YouTube, and Flickr for the sharing of photographs, and Wikipedia, the online encyclopaedia written by its users. There are, plainly, privacy costs to be incurred. The members of social networks may be blissfully unaware of the consequences of the widespread dissemination of their personal information. Providers should, of course, inform them on how to restrict access to these data. They ought to offer opt-out options for general profile data and opt-ins for sensitive data. Users need to know there is little or no protection against the copying of their personal data, whether or not these data relate to themselves or to others.

There are other privacy perils. Facebook, for example, allowed users to add gadgets to their profiles and play with third-party applications without leaving the Facebook site. But this gives rise to privacy problems. When a user installs a Facebook application, the application can see anything that the user can see. The application may therefore request information about the user, his or her friends, and fellow network members. There is nothing to stop the owner of the application from collecting, viewing—and misusing—this personal information. The Facebook terms of use agreement urges application developers to refrain from doing this, but Facebook has no way of discovering or preventing them from engaging in these activities.

However, under pressure from the Canadian Privacy Commissioner, it has recently amended its privacy policy so that applications cannot access users' friends' profile information without the express permission of each friend. Users generally regard their profiles on social networking sites simply as a form of self-expression, but the profiles have commercial value to marketing companies, competing networking sites, and identity thieves. The site has a history of continually changing its privacy settings. In 2010 founder Mark Zuckerberg declared that privacy was no longer a social norm. However, under pressure, it later announced the introduction of a 'privacy checkup' service to ensure users know when they are publicly sharing data. Facebook is also changing how users choose to whom their posts will be shown by moving the 'audience selector' to the top left of its iPhone app, and giving it greater prominence so that users can switch more easily between posts that are 'public' and those that are 'just for friends'.

Data mining is used mainly by corporations that seek to establish patterns of transactional and other behaviour by consumers. It may also include information about factors such as price, advertising competition, and customer demographics. So a retailer might employ point-of-sale records of purchases to target promotions based on an individual's purchasing history. By mining demographic data from loyalty cards, for instance, the retailer is able to develop products and promotions that appeal to explicit customers. Buy an item from Amazon and you will soon receive suggestions of similar products. Your selection is recorded, tracked, collated, and analysed. And this practice is increasingly used by retailers around the world.

While it is valuable in commercial, medical, or scientific contexts, data mining creates risks to privacy. It exposes information that would otherwise be hidden.

Chapter 6
The death of privacy?

'Privacy is dead. Get over it.' Thus spake Scott McNealy, CEO of Sun Microsystems in 1999. He is not alone; privacy's obituary has been written by a growing number of scholars and commentators. A requiem is, however, premature. The invaders are at the gate, but the citadel will not fall without a battle.

Vital signs

For many privacy advocates, privacy still lives and breathes—however, it requires urgent resuscitation. Groups such as Privacy International, the Electronic Frontier Foundation (EFF), the Electronic Privacy Information Center (EPIC), and several others continue to wage a gruelling campaign against the seemingly inexorable conquest of today's incarnation of Big Brother (see Figure 11). The battle has become especially challenging since the events of 11 September 2001, and the revelations in 2013 by Edward Snowden that exposed the scale of surveillance undertaken by the United States National Security Agency.

Examples abound. Fears of comprehensive 24-hour monitoring by CCTV were raised in early 2009 by the announcement that to safeguard security at the 2012 Olympic Games in London, the British government had appointed European Aeronautic Defense

**11. The chilling image from George Orwell's apocalyptic novel,
Nineteen Eighty-Four has come to signify any authoritarian, surveillance
society.**

and Security (EADS), to develop a system, known as Dynamic
Visual Networks (DYVINE), that would allow a central police
control room to tap in remotely to any CCTV network in London
and plot the information on a detailed 3D map. It would include
vehicle number-plate recognition cameras as well as private
networks, such as those operating in shopping centres and car
parks facilitating the tracking of suspects throughout the city.
Advanced computer intelligence systems would assist officers by
filtering out all but the most relevant CCTV feeds entering the
control room, thereby cutting the time normally spent scrambling
from one camera to the next.

The anxiety generated by systems such as this focuses on the
dangers posed to privacy by the manifold forms of electronic and
other forms of monitoring and intrusion described in Chapter 1.
But there is the equally disconcerting onslaught perpetuated by the
media in pursuit of sensationalist gossip discussed in Chapter 4.

The exponential growth of the Internet in our daily lives poses urgent challenges that can only multiply.

Technology and tranquillity

The pace of technological innovation will continue to increase. This will be accompanied by new and more insidious forms of encroachment on our private lives. But privacy is too fundamental a democratic value for it to be vanquished without a struggle. It is true that, especially in the face of real or perceived threats, many are disposed to trade their privacy for safety or security—even when it is demonstrated, for example, that the proliferation of CCTV cameras has achieved only limited success in curbing crime.

The erosion of privacy therefore tends to occur by quiescent accretion: through apathy, indifference, or tacit support for measures that are packaged as essential or appear innocuous. And we should not pretend that in our digital world the regulation of privacy-invading conduct will be unproblematic; far from it. Online privacy is bound to continue to be vulnerable to a wide range of attacks. Yet cyberspace is prone to some degree of control, not necessarily by law, but rather through its essential make-up, its 'code': software and hardware that constitutes cyberspace. That code, it is argued by Lessig, can either produce a place where freedom prevails or one of oppressive control. Indeed, commercial considerations increasingly render cyberspace susceptible to regulation; it has become a location in which conduct is more strongly controlled than in real space. In the end, he maintains, it is a matter for us to determine; the choice is one of architecture—what sort of code should govern cyberspace, and who will control it. And in this respect, the central legal issue is code. We need to choose the values and principles which should animate that code.

Our defences against these depredations will require also the political will to enact—and actively enforce—appropriate legislation and codes of conduct. Existing data-protection laws, where they exist, need constant revision and rejuvenation, and urgent enactment where they do not. The office of privacy or information commissioner requires adequate funding to facilitate the effective oversight of legislative and other threats to privacy, and the proper regulation and provision of advice and information. An appropriately funded, supported, and competent privacy commissioner can play an indispensable role as guardian of our personal data.

The collaboration of software and hardware manufacturers, service providers, and computer users, along with advice and information about how best to safeguard personal information, are critical components of any privacy protection strategy.

The importance of the PETs to counter PITs—described in Chapter 1—cannot be over-emphasized. Humans create technology. It can therefore both impair and improve our privacy. Firewalls, anti-hacking mechanisms, and other means are the first line of defence. Expressing one's privacy preferences (see Chapter 1) through, for example the Platform for Privacy Preferences (P3P) Project, is another vital tool in safeguarding our vanishing privacy. How does it work? The privacy preference settings panel of 'Privacy Bird', for example, allows you to configure your personal privacy preferences. When it encounters a website that does not match your privacy preferences, a red warning icon appears in your browser title bar. There are three pre-configured settings: low, medium, and high. When you select a setting, a tick or check mark materializes next to the specific items that will trigger warnings under that setting. The low setting generates a warning only at websites that may use health or medical information, or keep marketing or mailing lists from which you cannot be removed. The medium setting includes additional warnings when sites may share your personally identified information, or if a site does not permit you to establish what data they hold about you. The high setting triggers the maximum number of warnings.

Technological methods to facilitate such preferences are emerging, along with instruments by which data collectors are able to acquaint themselves with their responsibilities. Pressure groups, non-governmental organizations, lobbyists, and privacy advocates of every stripe perform a vital function in raising consciousness of the relentless assaults on privacy.

Rights online

While the extraordinary capacity of the Internet to collect, store, transfer, monitor, link, and match an incalculable amount of our personal information plainly poses considerable risks to our rights (see Box 10), technology is simultaneously our adversary and our ally.

Box 10 Internet privacy rights

'[W]e need internet privacy rights...to address the threats to our autonomy that arise through privacy-related problems on the internet...Some of the threats are clear and direct, some far more insidious, but deficiencies in the way our privacy is protected play a key role in all of them.' Four rights are identified:

1. A right to roam the internet with privacy

2. A right to monitor those who monitor us

3. A right to delete personal data

4. A right to an online identity

'The business sector is where what hope that there is appears to lie and where [these] rights...could play their most important role.'

P. Bernal, *Internet Privacy Rights: Rights to Protect Autonomy*

In addition to the seemingly insatiable appetite of law-enforcement and intelligence agencies for our personal information, commercial enterprises are no less voracious (see Box 10). But, as one commentator reminds us, there is a symbiotic relationship between consumers (who benefit from money-saving online services) and businesses (who rely on their capacity to collect and use our personal data).

Pursuing paparazzi

The appetite for tittle-tattle is unlikely to decline. It will continue to be fed—both offline and online—by unauthorized disclosures of personal information. The media in their print and digital manifestations, blogs, social networking sites, and other online purveyors of private facts, both voluntary and unsolicited, present intractable challenges to any form of regulation or control.

The power of the paparazzi shows few signs of diminishing. Though their intrusive conduct is often conflated with the publication of its fruits, there is a widespread recognition that the law is inadequate on both counts.

At least three possible solutions have been advanced. The first seeks to criminalize the activities of invasive journalists and photographers. So, for example, the state of California (whose constitution explicitly protects privacy) enacted an 'anti-paparazzi' law that creates tort liability for 'physical' and 'constructive' invasions of privacy through photographing, videotaping, or recording a person engaging in a 'personal or familial activity'.

A second line of attack attempts to cajole or compel the media to adopt a variety of forms of self-regulation. The protracted efforts, especially in Britain, to achieve this compromise, and so avert legislative controls, have met with little success. And even the beefed up body proposed by the Leveson Inquiry is unlikely to succeed in preventing or controlling the worst excesses of the media. The third approach is the enactment of legislation along the lines of the American tort of intentional intrusion upon the plaintiff's seclusion or solitude, or into his or her private affairs. Liability is distinct from that which may attach to the public disclosure, if any, of the information acquired as a result of the intrusion. This is a highly controversial solution, but one that merits serious consideration. Greater precision is required in respect of both the conception of 'private information' and the 'public interest'. In the case of the latter, there is a conspicuous need for clear, authoritative guidelines as to what sort of publications are incorporated within this otherwise nebulous notion.

But privacy warrants protection in its own right; backdoor remedies will, in the end, be counterproductive. The ideal answer is explicit, carefully drafted legislation that creates civil and criminal sanctions for seriously offensive, intentional, or reckless intrusion into an individual's solitude or seclusion, and the unauthorized publication of personal information. The latter is, of course, always to be balanced against freedom of speech, as discussed in Chapter 4.

There are two typical responses to a legislative solution. The first claims that it represents political interference with free speech. This is unpersuasive; it could apply equally to any statute that touched on public order, defamation, obscenity, contempt of court, blasphemy, copyright, hate speech, and so on. The second contention is that a privacy statute could become outdated quickly, would not allow for flexibility on a case-by-case basis, and could generate greater litigation over its interpretation. Again, this argument is specious since it assumes that legislation is immune to amendment, that it would be formulated in elaborate, intricate terms, and that the impact of legislation on judicial interpretation is not a scientific exercise.

The increasing complexity of the challenge faced by the courts in mediating between privacy and free speech renders the subject a perfect candidate for the creation of a statutory tort. Moreover, the relationship between privacy and freedom of speech is far too important a constitutional question to be left to the vagaries and potential self-interest of the media.

Conclusion

There is no simple answer. Government surveillance relentlessly intensifies (see Figure 12). The real issue is whether, as appears to be the case, the interests of the individual are to be sacrificed at the altar of an often contrived 'public interest'? The law, of course, should be a last resort. Non-legal regulatory forms of

12. Striking street art attributed to Banksy near the British intelligence agency GCHQ in the wake of the storm over UK and US surveillance revealed by Edward Snowden.

mediation will, in some cases, satisfy a victim's grievance. Nor should the recognition of appropriate, privacy-respecting rights online, be neglected. Sensitivity to cruel disclosures of intimate information posted on social networks and blogs must become a vital element of moral responsibility. Schools should ensure that pupils appreciate the perils of malevolent and petulant posts, as well as those that disclose individuals' own intimate details which (they must be warned) are normally permanent and can be effortlessly re-broadcast by third parties—including, of course, the media. The 'architecture' of the web can significantly enhance privacy. Default settings of social media need to be clearly and visibly set in favour of privacy.

The Internet has radically changed not only how we communicate, educate, transact, and present ourselves; it is an environment that most of us increasingly inhabit—voluntarily or inescapably—in which our very identity may be transformed and distorted. Potential employers, at the click of a mouse, can unearth details of an applicant that may be obsolete, erroneous, or irrelevant, although in Europe at least the 'right to be forgotten' may, in some cases, eradicate its immutability. The potential for the misuse of sensitive information has dramatically escalated. Yet, despite this transformation, we need to recall what has *not* changed. The values that we prize in a free society including, of course, privacy and the freedom of the media, are both enhanced and endangered by the digital revolution. It is these values—though their survival is sustained by social norms—that occasionally require the sustenance and defence of the law.

Neither at work nor at home are we entitled to assume that our online applications are safe. We must look to both technology and the law to provide shelter. Technology, it has been frequently stated, generates both the malady and part of the cure. And while the law is rarely an adequate tool against the dedicated intruder, the advances in protective software along with the fair information practices adopted by the European Directive and the laws of several jurisdictions, afford a rational and sound normative framework for the collection, use, and transfer of personal data. It offers a pragmatic analysis of the uses to which personal information is actually put, the manner of its collection, and the legitimate expectations of individuals. But it—and the law, ethics, and practice—stands in need of constant review and modification if privacy is to survive as a right to which we can continue to lay claim.

References

Chapter 1: Privacy in peril

M. Foucault, *Discipline and Punish: The Birth of the Prison* (Harmondsworth: Penguin, 1991).

G. Orwell, *Nineteen Eighty-Four* (Harmondsworth: Penguin Classics, 2013), p. 100.

'[W]e have left the big data era…': P. Tucker, *The Naked Future: What Happens in a World that Anticipates Your Every Move?* (New York: Penguin, 2014), pp. xiv–xv.

'It was reported in early 2009…': *Sunday Times*, 4 January 2009.

'Free conversation is often characterized…': L.B. Schwartz, 'On Current Proposals to Legalize Wiretapping' (1954) 103 *University of Pennsylvania Law Review*, p. 162.

'These companies track one's every keystroke…': D. Rosen, *Four ways your privacy is being invaded*, <http://www.salon.com/2012/09/11/four_ways_your_privacy_is_being_invaded/>.

'[E]xamples of characteristics on which biometric technologies can be based…': drawn from Roger Clarke, 'Biometrics and Privacy', <http://www.rogerclarke.com/DV/Biometrics.html>.

'[A] bit more invasive than a security guard…': L. Lessig, *Code and Other Laws of Cyberspace* (New York: Basic Books, 1999), p. 194.

'Imagine if a hacker put together information…': E.G. Lush, 'How Cyber-Crime Became a Multi-Billion-Pound Industry', *The Spectator*, 16 June 2007.

Chapter 2: An enduring value

My attempt to address the intractable problem of defining privacy draws on my serial endeavours to grasp this nettle; some of these works are listed in the Further reading section.

'The closer people come...': R. Sennett, *The Fall of Public Man* (Harmondsworth: Penguin, 1974), p. 338.

'In ancient feeling...': H. Arendt, *The Human Condition* (Chicago: University of Chicago Press, 1958), p. 38.

'[L]iberalism may be said largely...': S. Lukes, *Individualism* (Oxford: Basil Blackwell, 1973), p. 62.

'One of the central goals...': M. Horwitz, 'The History of the Public/Private Distinction' (1982) 130 *University of Pennsylvania Law Review*, p. 1424.

'[T]he sole end...': J.S. Mill, *On Liberty* (London: Longman, Roberts & Green, 1869), p. 9.

'[W]hat if we all behaved...': D. Eggers, *The Circle* (London: Hamish Hamilton, 2013), p. 290.

'On any given day...': A.F. Westin, *Privacy and Freedom* (New York: Atheneum, 1967), pp. 34–5.

'[A]n air of injured gentility': H. Kalven, 'Privacy in Tort Law: Were Warren and Brandeis Wrong?' (1966) 31 *Law and Contemporary Problems*, p. 329.

'The "claim of individuals, groups..."': A.F. Westin, *Privacy and Freedom* (New York: Atheneum, 1967), p. 7.

'To the extent that people conceal...': R. Posner, 'The Right of Privacy' (1978) 123 *Georgia Law Review*, p. 401.

'[P]rivacy consists of "limited accessibility"...': R. Gavison, 'Privacy and the Limits of Law' (1980) 89 *Yale Law Journal* 412.

Chapter 3: A legal right

Prince Albert v Strange (1849) 1H. & W. 1. 64 E.R. 293. On appeal: (1849) 1 Mac. & G. 25, 41 E.R. 1171.

S.D. Warren and L.D. Brandeis, 'The Right to Privacy' (1890) 5 *Harvard Law Review* 196.

'Flour of the family': *Roberson v Rochester Folding Box Co.* 171 N.Y. 538; 64 N.E. 442 (1902).

'[T]he Supreme Court of Georgia...': *Pavesich v New England Life Insurance Co.*, 122 Ga. 190; 50 S.E. 68 (1905).

'[N]ot one of tort, "but a complex of four ... "': W.L. Prosser, 'Privacy'
  (1960) 48 *California Law Review* 383.

'[I]ts moral basis as an aspect of human dignity': E.J. Bloustein,
  'Privacy as an Aspect of Human Dignity: An Answer to Dean
  Prosser' (1964) 39 *New York University Law Review* 962.

'[G]iven the legal mind's ...': H. Kalven, 'Privacy in Tort Law: Were
  Warren and Brandeis Wrong?' (1966) 31 *Law and Contemporary
  Problems* 326.

Olmstead v United States 277 U.S. 438 (1928).

Katz v United States 398 U.S. 347 (1967).

Griswold v Connecticut 381 U.S. 479 (1965).

Roe v Wade 410 U.S. 113 (1973).

'[U]ndoubtedly the best-known case ...' and 'The war between ...':
  R. Dworkin, *Life's Dominion: An Argument about Abortion and
  Euthanasia* (London: Harper Collins, 1993), pp. 4 and 103.

Bowers v Hardwick 478 U.S. 186 (1986).

Lawrence v Texas 539 U.S. 558 (2003).

'In 1972, the Younger Committee ...': *Report of the Committee on
  Privacy* (Chairman: K. Younger), Cmnd 5012 (1972) Para. 653.

Douglas v Hello! Ltd [2007] 2 W.L.R. 920 (H.L.).

'[C]oming into force of the ...': Lord Hoffmann: *Wainwright v Home
  Office* [2003] U.K.H.L. 53, Para. 34.

'[T]he final impetus to the recognition of a right of privacy ...':
  Douglas v Hello! Ltd [2005] 1 Q.B. 967 at para 111, *per* Sedley LJ.

Australian Broadcasting Corporation v Lenah Game Meats Pty Ltd
  [2001] HCA 63.

Hosking v Runting and Pacific Magazines NZ Ltd [2004] CA 101.

Gaskin v United Kingdom (1989) 12 E.H.H.R. 36.

Leander v Sweden (1987) 9 E.H.H.R. 443.

Katz v United States 389 U.S. 347 (1967).

'[T]he party to the conversation who secretly ...': *Privacy*, Australian
  Law Reform Commission No. 22, Para. 1128.

Klass v Federal Republic of Germany (1978) 2 E.H.H.R 214.

Malone v United Kingdom (1984) 7 E.H.R.R. 14.

Kennedy v United Kingdom (2010) E.C.H.R. 682 (18 May 2010).

'[N]ot because we wish to hamper ...': S.M. Beck, 'Electronic
  Surveillance and the Administration of Criminal Justice' (1968)
  46 *Canadian Bar Review*, p. 687.

Chapter 4: Privacy and freedom of expression

Some of the discussion on the attempt to reconcile privacy and
freedom of expression is based on my *Privacy and Press Freedom*
(London: Blackstone, 1995), and *Privacy and Media Freedom*
(Oxford: Oxford University Press, 2014).

Campbell v Mirror Group Newspapers Ltd [2004] 2A.C. 457 (H.L.)

'[P]hotography or video devices…': *Douglas v Hello! Ltd* [2006]
Q.B. 125; [2007] 2 W.L.R. 920 (H.L.).

'contributed to a debate of…' and 'sought seclusion': *Von Hannover v
Germany* [2004] E.M.L.R. 379 (E.C.H.R.)

'[T]he clearest message…': *An Inquiry into the Culture, Practices and
Ethics of the Press*, HC 780 (2012), para. 4.7, p. 739.

'Even if gossip…': J. Rosen, *The Unwanted Gaze: The Destruction of
Privacy in America* (New York: Random House, 2000), p. 205.

'[M]ore comprehensive scheme…' and '[A]t most points the law…':
T.L. Emerson, *The System of Freedom of Expression* (New York:
Random House, 1970).

'[A] rigorous examination of motives…': E. Barendt, *Freedom of
Speech*, 2nd edn. (Oxford: Oxford University Press, 2005), p. 24.

'And though all the winds of doctrine…': J. Milton, *Areopagitica*
(1644) (Macmillan, 1914).

'[S]uffers from a failure…': F. Schauer, *Free Speech: A Philosophical
Enquiry* (Cambridge: Cambridge University Press, 1982), p. 56.

'The principle of the freedom of speech…': A. Meiklejohn, *Political
Freedom: The Constitutional Powers of the People* (New York:
Oxford University Press, 1965).

'The liberty of the press is indeed essential…': W. Blackstone,
4 *Commentaries on the Laws of England* (1769), pp. 151–2.

New York Times v Sullivan 376 U.S. 254 at p. 270 per Brennan J (1964).

Time, Inc. v Hill 385 U.S. 374 (1967).

'[S]o long as the interest of privacy…': T. Emerson, *Towards a
General Theory of the First Amendment* (New York: Vintage,
1966), p. 75.

'It cannot be too strongly emphasized…': *R v Central Independent
Television PLC* [1994] Fam. 192 at p. 203 per Hoffmann LJ (as he
then was).

'[E]xceptional cases, where the intended…' and 'Blackstone was
concerned to prevent…': *Schering Chemicals Ltd v Falkman*
[1982] 1 Q.B. 1 at p. 18 per Lord Denning M.R., and p. 39, per
Lord Templeman, respectively.

'[A]t some point the public interest...': *Sidis v F.-R. Publishing Co.* 34F. Supp. 19 (S.D.N.Y., 1938); 113F. 2d. 806 at p 809 (1940).

Restatement (Second) of the Law of Torts, §652D (b) and comment h.

Sipple v Chronicle Publishing Co. 201 Cal. Rptr 665 (1984).

Diaz v Oakland Tribune Inc. 118 Cal. Rptr 762 at p. 773 (1983).

Ann-Margret v High Society Magazine, Inc. 498F. Supp. 401 at p. 405 (1980).

'[D]eference to the judgment...': D.L. Zimmerman, 'Requiem for a Heavyweight: A Farewell to Warren and Brandeis's Privacy Tort' (1983) 68 *Cornell Law Review* 291, p. 353.

Melvin v Reid 112 Cal. App. 285; 297P. 91 (1931).

Sidis v F.-R. Publishing Corporation Sidis v F.-R. Publishing Co. 34F. Supp. 19 (S.D.N.Y., 1938); 113F. 2d. 806.

Time, Inc. v Hill 385 U.S. 374, p. 388 (1967).

Chapter 5: Data protection

'Recently the European...': *I v Finland* Eur. Ct. H.R., No. 20511/03 (17 July 2008).

Eastweek Publisher Ltd v The Privacy Commissioner for Personal Data [2000] H.K.C. 692.

'Perhaps because of its very lack of teeth...': J.B. Rule, *Privacy in Peril* (Oxford University Press, 2007), p. 138.

'European and other countries...': N. Witzleb, D. Lindsay, M. Paterson, S. Rodrick (eds), *Emerging Challenges in Privacy Law: Comparative Perspectives* (Cambridge University Press, 2014).

Chapter 6: The death of privacy?

L. Lessig, *Code and Other Laws of Cyberspace* (New York: Basic Books, 1999).

Platform for Privacy Preferences (P3P) Project: <http://www.w3.org/P3P/>.

'[We] need internet privacy rights...': P. Bernal, *Internet Privacy Rights: Rights to Protect Autonomy* (Cambridge University Press, 2014), pp. 15 ff and 263.

Privacy Bird: <http://www.privacybird.org>.

Electronic Privacy Information Center (EPIC): <https://epic.org/reports/prettypoorprivacy.html>.

Further reading

The subject of privacy has attracted the attention of scholars from a wide variety of disciplines, including philosophy, sociology, political science, and law. To avoid swamping the reader with an impossibly vast list of sources, I have restricted this inventory to reasonable—and accessible—proportions, omitting references to the prodigious quantity of periodical literature that grapples with this kaleidoscopic concept (the most essential of which are cited in the References section).

Chapter 1: Privacy in peril

D. Amerland, *The Social Media Mind: How Social Media is Changing Business, Politics and Science and Helps Create a New World Order* (Marietta, GA: New Line Publishing, 2012).

J. Angwin, *Dragnet Nation: A Quest for Privacy, Security, and Freedom in a World of Relentless Surveillance* (New York: Times Books, 2014).

Y. Benkler, *The Wealth of Networks: How Social Production Transforms Markets and Freedom* (Stanford, CA: Stanford Law Books, 2007).

P. Bernal, *Internet Privacy Rights: Rights to Protect Autonomy* (Cambridge: Cambridge University Press, 2014).

J. Brenner, *Glass Houses: Privacy, Secrecy, and Cyber Insecurity in a Transparent World* (Harmondsworth: Penguin, 2013).

N. Christakis and J. Fowler, *Connected: The Surprising Power of Our Social Networks and How They Shape Our Lives. How Your Friends' Friends' Friends Affect Everything You Feel, Think, and Do* (New York: Back Bay Books, 2011).

T.H. Davenport, *Big Data at Work: Dispelling the Myths, Uncovering the Opportunities* (Harvard, MA: Harvard Business Review Press, 2014).

J. Goldsmith and T. Wu, *Who Controls the Internet? Illusions of a Borderless World* (Oxford: Oxford University Press, 2006).

G. Greenwald, *No Place to Hide: Edward Snowden, the NSA, and the U.S. Surveillance State* (New York: Metropolitan Books, 2014).

L. Harding, *The Snowden Files: The Inside Story of the World's Most Wanted Man* (London: Vintage, 2014).

D. Lyon, *Surveillance after September 11* (Cambridge: Polity Press, 2003).

V. Mayer-Schönberger and K. Cukier, *Big Data: A Revolution that Will Transform How We Live, Work, and Think* (New York: Eamon Dolan/Mariner Books, 2014).

J.K. Petersen, *Understanding Surveillance Technologies: Spy Devices, Privacy, History and Applications* (Boca Raton, FL: Auerbach, 2007).

L. Rainie and B. Wellman, *Networked: The New Social Operating System* (Harvard MA: The MIT Press, 2012).

J.B. Rule, *Privacy in Peril* (New York: Oxford University Press, 2007).

B. Schouten, N.C. Juul, A. Drygajlo, and M. Tistarelli (eds), *Biometrics and Identity Management* (Heidelberg: Springer, 2008).

R. Scoble and S. Israel, *Age of Context: Mobile, Sensors, Data and the Future of Privacy* (Seattle, WA: CreateSpace Independent Publishing Platform, 2013).

D.J. Solove, *The Digital Person: Technology and Privacy in the Information Age* (New York: New York University Press, 2004).

M. Taylor, *Genetic Data and the Law: A Critical Perspective on Privacy Protection* (Cambridge: Cambridge University Press, 2012).

P. Tucker, *The Naked Future: What Happens in a World that Anticipates Your Every Move?* (New York: Penguin, 2014).

N. Witzleb, D. Lindsay, M. Paterson, and S. Rodrick (eds), *Emerging Challenges in Privacy Law: Comparative Perspectives* (Cambridge: Cambridge University Press, 2014).

Chapter 2: An enduring value

Anita Allen, *Unpopular Privacy: What Must We Hide?* (New York: Oxford University Press, 2011).

A. Lever, *On Privacy* (London: Routledge, 2012).

A. Etzioni, *The Limits of Privacy* (New York: Basic Books, 1999).

J. Griffin, *On Human Rights* (Oxford: Oxford University Press, 2008).

J. Inness, *Privacy, Intimacy and Isolation* (New York: Oxford University Press, 1992).

L. Lessig, *Code: Version 2.0* (New York: Basic Books, 2006).

A. Moore, *Privacy Rights: Moral and Legal Foundations* (Philadelphia, PA: University of Pennsylvania Press, 2009).

B. Moore Jr, *Privacy: Studies in Social and Cultural History*, 3rd edn (London: Routledge, 1984).

H. Nissenbaum, *Privacy in Context: Technology, Policy, and the Integrity of Social Life* (Stanford: Stanford Law Books, 2009).

F. Schoeman (ed.), *Philosophical Dimensions of Privacy: An Anthology* (Cambridge: Cambridge University Press, 1984).

C. Shirky, *Here Comes Everybody: The Power of Organizing Without Organizations* (Harmondsworth: Penguin, 2009).

D.J. Solove, *Nothing to Hide: The False Tradeoff between Privacy and Security* (New Haven: Yale University Press, 2013).

R. Wacks, *Law, Morality, and the Private Domain* (Hong Kong: Hong Kong University Press, 2000).

R. Wacks (ed.), *Privacy: The International Library of Essays in Law and Legal Theory*. Volume I: *The Concept of Privacy* (New York: New York University Press, 1993).

A.F. Westin, *Privacy and Freedom* (New York: Atheneum, 1967).

Chapter 3: A legal right

D.J. Harris, M. O'Boyle, C. Warbrick, and E. Bates (eds), *Law of the European Convention on Human Rights*, 2nd edn (Oxford: Oxford University Press, 2009).

A.T. Kenyon and M. Richardson (eds), *New Dimensions in Privacy Law: International and Comparative Perspectives* (Cambridge: Cambridge University Press, 2006).

J.L. Mills, *Privacy: The Lost Right* (New York: Oxford University Press, 2008).

J.B. Rule and G. Greenleaf (eds), *Global Privacy Protection: The First Generation* (London: Edward Elgar, 2008).

D.J. Solove and P.M. Schwartz, *Privacy Law Fundamentals*, 2nd edn (Portsmouth, NH: IAPP, 2013).

R. Wacks, *Personal Information: Privacy and the Law* (Oxford: Clarendon Press, 1989).

R. Wacks (ed.), *Privacy: The International Library of Essays in Law and Legal Theory*. Volume II: *Privacy and the Law* (New York: New York University Press, 1993).

R. Wacks, *The Protection of Privacy* (London: Sweet & Maxwell, 1980).

Chapter 4: Privacy and freedom of expression

L. Alexander, *Is There a Right of Freedom of Expression?* (Cambridge: Cambridge University Press, 2005).

E. Barendt, *Freedom of Speech*, 2nd edn (Oxford: Oxford University Press, 2007).

C. Calvert, *Voyeur Nation: Media, Privacy, and Peering in Modern Culture* (New York: Basic Books, 2004).

T.L. Emerson, 'The Right of Privacy and Freedom of the Press' (1979) 14 *Harvard Civil Rights-Civil Liberties Law Review* 329.

H. Jenkins, *Convergence Culture: Where Old and New Media Collide* (New York: New York University Press, 2008).

N. Moreham, M. Warby, and I. Christie (eds), *Tugendhat and Christie: The Law of Privacy and the Media*, 2nd edn (Oxford: Oxford University Press, 2011).

J. Rozenberg, *Privacy and the Press* (Oxford: Oxford University Press, 2005).

D.J. Solove, *The Future of Reputation: Gossip, Rumor, and Privacy on the Internet* (New Haven, CT: Yale University Press, 2007).

H. Tomlinson, *Privacy and the Media: The Developing Law* (London: Matrix Chambers, 2002).

R. Wacks, *Privacy and Press Freedom* (London: Blackstone Press, 1995).

R. Wacks, *Privacy and Media Freedom* (Oxford: Oxford University Press, 2013).

D.L. Zimmerman, 'Requiem for a Heavyweight: A Farewell to Warren and Brandeis's Privacy Tort' (1983) 68 *Cornell Law Review* 291.

Chapter 5: Data protection

C. Bennett, *Regulating Privacy: Data Protection and Public Policy in Europe and the United States* (Ithaca, NY: Cornell University Press, 1992).

C. Bennett and C. Raab, *The Governance of Privacy: Policy*

Instruments in Global Perspective, 2nd edn (Cambridge, MA: MIT Press, 2006).

M. Berthold and R. Wacks, *Hong Kong Data Privacy Law: Territorial Regulation in a Borderless World*, 2nd edn (Hong Kong: Sweet & Maxwell Asia, 2003).

L.A. Bygrave, *Data Protection Law: Approaching its Rationale, Logic and Limits* (The Hague: Kluwer Law International, 2002).

L.A. Bygrave, *Data Privacy Law: An International Perspective* (New York: Oxford University Press, 2014).

G. Greenleaf, *Asian Data Privacy Laws: Trade and Human Rights Perspectives* (Oxford: Oxford University Press, 2014).

P. Schwartz and J. Reidenberg, *Data Protection Law: A Study of United States Data Protection* (Dayton: Michie, 1996).

Chapter 6: The death of privacy?

S. Garfinkel, *Database Nation: The Death of Privacy in the Twenty-First Century* (Sebastopol, CA: O'Reilly, 2000).

S. Gutwirth, *Privacy and the Information Age* (Lanham, MD: Rowman & Littlefield, 2002).

B. Kahin and C. Nesson (eds), *Borders in Cyberspace: Information Policy and the Global Information Infrastructure* (Cambridge, MA: MIT Press, 1997).

G. Laurie, *Genetic Privacy: A Challenge to Medico-Legal Norms* (Cambridge: Cambridge University Press, 2002).

D. Lyon, C. Bennett, and R. Grant (eds), *Visions of Privacy: Policy Choices for the Digital Age* (Toronto: University of Toronto Press, 1998).

K. O'Hara and N. Shadbolt, *The Spy in the Coffee Machine: The End of Privacy as We Know It* (Oxford: Oneworld, 2008).

J. Rosen, *The Unwanted Gaze: The Destruction of Privacy in America* (New York: Random House, 2000).

C.J. Sykes, *The End of Privacy* (London: St Martin's Press, 2000).

J. Zittrain, *The Future of the Internet: And How to Stop It* (London: Allen Lane, 2008).

Websites

Electronic Privacy Information Center (EPIC) <www.epic.org>.
Privacy International <www.privacyinternational.org>.

The Privacy Surgeon <www.privacysurgeon.org>.
Privacy Rights Clearinghouse <www.privacyrights.org>.
American Civil Liberties Union <www.aclu.org>.
Roger Clarke's Dataveillance and Information Privacy Pages
    <www.anu.edu.au/people/Roger.Clarke/DV>.
Electronic Frontier Foundation (EFF) <www.eff.org>.
Health Privacy Project (HPP) <www.healthprivacy.org>.
Anti-Phishing Working Group (APWG) <www.antiphishing.org>.
The Privacy Forum <privacy@vortex.com>.
Institute for the Study of Privacy Issues (ISPI) <www.PrivacyNews.com>.
Medical Privacy Coalition <www.medicalprivacycoalition.org>.
People for Internet Responsibility (PFIR) <www.pfir.org>.
Privacy News and Information <www.privacy.org>.
World Privacy Forum <www.worldprivacyforum.org>.
Article 19 <http://www.article19.org/>.

Index

LAW
A Very Short Introduction
Raymond Wacks

Law underlies our society - it protects our rights, imposes duties on each of us, and establishes a framework for the conduct of almost every social, political, and economic activity. The punishment of crime, compensation of the injured, and the enforcement of contracts are merely some of the tasks of a modern legal system. It also strives to achieve justice, promote freedom, and protect our security. This *Very Short Introduction* provides a clear, jargon-free account of modern legal systems, explaining how the law works both in the Western tradition and around the world.